Unified Business Laws for Africa:
Common Law Perspectives on OHADA

GLOBAL MARKET BRIEFINGS

Unified Business Laws for Africa: Common Law Perspectives on OHADA

Martha Simo Tumnde, née Njikam
Mohammed Baba Idris
Jean Alain Penda M.
John Ademola Yakubu
Claire Moore Dickerson

Edited by
Claire Moore Dickerson

GMB

28/7/09

Publishers' note

Every possible effort has been made to ensure that the information contained in this publication is accurate at the time of going to press and neither the publishers nor any of the authors, editors, contributors or sponsors can accept responsibility for any errors or omissions, however caused. No responsibility for loss or damage occasioned to any person acting, or refraining from action, as a result of the material in this publication can be accepted by the editors, authors, the publisher or any of the contributors or sponsors.

Users and readers of this publication may copy or download portions of the material herein for personal use, and may include portions of this material in internal reports and/or reports to customers, and on an occasional and infrequent basis individual articles from the material, provided that such articles (or portions of articles) are attributed to this publication by name, the individual contributor of the portion used and GMB Publishing Ltd.

Users and readers of this publication shall not reproduce, distribute, display, sell, publish, broadcast, repurpose, or circulate the material to any third party, or create new collective works for resale or for redistribution to servers or lists, or reuse any copyrighted component of this work in other works, without the prior written permission of GMB Publishing Ltd.

GMB Publishing Ltd.
Hereford House
23 – 24 Smithfield Street
London EC1A 9LF
United Kingdom

525 South 4th Street, #241
Philadelphia, PA 19147
United States of America

www.gmbpublishing.com

This edition first published 2009 by GMB Publishing Ltd.

Hardcopy ISBN 978-1-84673-150-1
E-book ISBN 978-1-84673-151-8

British Library Cataloguing in Publication Data

A CIP record for this book is available from the British Library

Library of Congress Cataloguing-in Publication Data

Typeset by David Lewis XML Associates Ltd.
Printed and bound in Great Britain and the USA by Lightning Source.

Contents

About the Authors

Martha Simo Tumnde, née Njikam, Dean of the Faculty of Social and Management Sciences and Associate Professor at the University of Buea, Cameroon, previously served as its first Head of Department of Law, and before that taught law at the University of Yaounde. Her area of specialisation is commercial/business law with a strong research interest in comparative law. She has published widely in these fields. She is a Barrister and Solicitor at the Supreme Court of Cameroon. She earned her LLB from Liverpool University, LLM from the University of London and PhD from the University of Sheffield.

Mohammed Baba Idris is a Judge of the Federal High Court in Nigeria, and is also an associate member of the Chartered Institute of Arbitrators (UK). He received his LLM from the University of Lagos, an LLB in Common and Islamic Laws from the Usmanu Danfodio University in Sokoto, and the Barrister at Law certificate from the Nigerian Law School in Lagos. His practice specialties included maritime law, oil and gas law, international trade law and commercial litigation. He was counsel in leading law firms in Nigeria including Chief Rotimi Williams Chambers and Fidelis Oditah & Co., and also served as Head of the Legal and Chartering departments of Oando Supply & Trading Company Limited, the leading oil trading company in Nigeria.

Jean Alain Penda Matipé is Cameroonian. He holds an LLB from the University of Buéa (Cameroon) and an LLM in International Corporate and Financial Law from the University of Wolverhampton. He is currently a researcher at Global Sales Law in Switzerland while earning his doctorate at the University of Basel. Author of several articles on OHADA law, Mr. Penda is also a member of UNIDA (Association for the Unification of Business Law in Africa), which he assists in matters involving English and Portuguese speaking countries worldwide.

The late **John Ademola Yakubu** was Professor of Law and a long-time member of the Faculty of Law of the University of Ibadan, where he specialized in Private International Law. He served also as the Honourable Attorney-General and Commissioner for Justice of Nigeria's Oyo State. He obtained his PhD from Obafemi Awolowo University (then the

University of Ife), Ile Ife, and did a post-doctoral fellowship at the University of London. He was a member of the African Society of International and Comparative Law based in London, the Nigerian Society of International Law, Nigerian Association of Law Teachers and a member of the Nigerian Bar Association.

Claire Moore Dickerson is the Sen. John B. Breaux Professor of Law at Tulane University in New Orleans, LA, USA. She earned her JD from Columbia University School of Law, and an LLM in Taxation from New York University School of Law, both in New York, NY, USA. Before teaching, she was a partner in the international law firm of Coudert Brothers where she specialised in international commercial transactions. Her scholarship has applied socioeconomic principles to business--related areas of law, with a particular focus on standards of performance, in both US and international contexts.

Foreword

OHADA is a system of business laws uniform across 16, soon 17 West and Central African countries. Even among the English-speaking, common law–trained legal professionals within its territory, 'OHADA' no longer is merely an acronym for the French words 'l'Organisation pour l'harmonisation en Afrique du droit des affaires' (in English, the Organization for the Harmonization in Africa of Business Law). Instead, 'OHADA' has become a proper noun, sometimes used adjectively as well.

OHADA also is a living organism. As this book goes to press, a proposed revision of the 1993 treaty has been signed by the heads of state and is beginning the ratification process. This revision honors OHADA's 15 years of existence and reflects the ten years of experience garnered since the first of its statutes, its Uniform Acts, became effective. The proposed updates recognise the supranational organization's legal and political realities and seek to enhance OHADA's ability to facilitate business transactions into and throughout the region.

To return to the genesis, OHADA exists because of the bold foresight of a few and the move by many towards integration. Chief among those few is the late Judge Kéba Mbaye, former Supreme Court Justice of Senegal and Vice-President of the International Court of Justice in The Hague. As the waves of independence washed over the African continent, Judge Mbaye sought to convince governments of the newly sovereign countries to adopt a uniform legal regime. He was not successful at that time, but he pursued his vision and in 1993, the treaty creating OHADA was signed.

Judge Mbaye was a norm entrepreneur. Even the clearest vision and most deserving cause will not succeed, however, if others will not follow. Two trends contributed to the realization of Judge Mbaye's dream. First, West and Central Africa suffered a financial crisis starting in the mid-late 1980s, forcing the region's political leaders to look for solutions, including a means of encouraging trade by reducing transaction costs. OHADA and its clear and sophisticated business laws, implemented by a supranational judicial system designed to promote predictability and transparency, and uniform across all member states, suddenly became very appealing. Second, and at least as important, Judge Mbaye and OHADA's other early supporters tapped into the rich vein of African integration.

In the first chapter, Professor John Ademola Yakubu places OHADA in the context of other integrating organizations on the continent. Before his untimely death, Professor Yakubu had proved himself a visionary in the same mould as Judge Mbaye. While many lawyers, judges and academics from countries of common law tradition were dismissing OHADA as too civilian for consideration, Professor Yakubu took the time to learn about OHADA and became convinced that the quality of its laws and of its supranational court, and the importance of encouraging cross-border transactions, together made OHADA an important tool for economic development. Professor Yakubu, a professor of law at the University of Ibadan in Nigeria, became a thoroughly knowledgeable and highly skilled champion of OHADA even though the OHADA treaty and laws are in French, and he did not speak French. Using translations of the OHADA texts, together with his thorough appreciation of common law principles in Nigeria and the United Kingdom, Professor Yakubu wrote, spoke and networked to encourage jurists of the Anglo-Saxon legal tradition to take a long and hard but unprejudiced look at OHADA. We are among his many colleagues who miss his passion and wisdom, and we dedicate this volume to his memory.

Continuing along the same vein, the second chapter describes Africa's long progression towards legal integration and situates OHADA in that trend. Jean Alain Penda Matipé, a graduate in law of the University of Buea in Cameroon, has earned an LLM at the University of Wolverhampton in the United Kingdom, specializing in business and financial law. Researcher at Global Sales Law in Switzerland, he is now earning his doctorate at the University of Basel. He is a regular consultant for UNIDA, a non-governmental organization chaired first by Judge Mbaye until his death, and now by the former president of OHADA's supranational court, Judge Seydou Ba. Mr Penda has been instrumental in disseminating information about OHADA both within member countries and to jurists in neighbouring jurisdictions.

In Chapter 3, the Honourable Justice Mohammed Baba Idris offers a comprehensive overview of OHADA's laws and structure. Justice Idris, now on the Federal High Court in Nigeria, was long a Barrister at the Nigerian bar. In that capacity, his clients' cross-border transactions took him to neighbouring countries, and there he encountered OHADA. As he relates the story, every time he enquired about local law applicable to a particular business topic, the answer was, 'OHADA'. After this had happened a few times and in more than one country, he concluded that he needed to understand OHADA in order to represent his clients properly. The result of his study is this remarkable, succinct and dispassionate review of OHADA's laws and institutions.

Dr Martha Simo Tumnde, née Njikam, gives us the next two chapters. She is Dean of the Faculty of Social and Management Sciences and Associate Professor at the University of Buea, the only purely anglophone university in Cameroon. Her early legal training was in the common law, and her PhD from the University of Sheffield in the United Kingdom was on comparative law. Her Chapter 4 offers a description of the OHADA laws and structures, including a discussion of significant changes now under consideration, from a unique perspective. Not only is she a jurist trained in the Anglo-Saxon legal tradition, but she lives and works in Cameroon's anglophone region, the only part of OHADA's territory that is not a civil law jurisdiction.

As she notes, her sector of Cameroon initially was resistant to OHADA. While she herself was an early objector as well, she took the time to study OHADA; how to teach the law of her country if she did not know it herself? In that process she became convinced of OHADA's potential: its laws and institutions are technically sophisticated, its institutional structures are designed to increase transparency and predictability and its laws' uniformity across national borders produce savings of both time and expenditure. The anglophone members of the Cameroonian national bar association took to calling her, with much admiration, 'Madame OHADA'. She has spoken extensively on OHADA in multiple venues, both in Europe and across Africa.

In her second contribution, Chapter 5, Dr Tumnde chooses a few topics that anglophone jurists in Cameroon, based on their unique experience, have identified as particular obstacles to OHADA's application in jurisdictions of Anglo-Saxon legal heritage. After describing procedural reasons for her common law colleagues' wariness about OHADA, she discusses the single most important complaint voiced by her colleagues: under the OHADA treaty, French has been the only working language of OHADA, and will continue to be so unless and until a treaty revision, now under consideration, is adopted. She also considers implementation issues both entirely within the OHADA institutional framework, for example concerning the supranational court, and also at the transition between the OHADA institutions' responsibilities and those of the national governments, for example with respect to the organization and functioning of the official registries.

Professor Yakubu provides Chapter 6 on simplified recovery procedures and measures of execution. This subject, and the OHADA law on the topic, deserve a separate chapter: if judgements and arbitral awards are not enforced, the rest of the laws and structures ultimately are irrelevant. In addition, because the subject is exactly at the boundary between OHADA's decision-making authority and the national governments' obligation to enforce those decisions, it also serves as a model for other issues that straddle the jurisdictions. Professor Yakubu enriches his explanation of the OHADA realities by comparing its statute to a common law analogue, namely Nigeria's law and practice.

In the final offering, Chapter 7, I glean hints about the future from OHADA's trajectory so far. OHADA's evolution is accelerating: as this book goes to press a major treaty-revision, signed in late 2008, is circulating for signature, and a ninth Uniform Act, this one concerning cooperatives, is expected to be adopted within a matter of months. My own background includes academic research on business laws, among which OHADA's laws, preceded by years of private, international commercial-corporate practice. Preparation specific to this project included time spent in various OHADA member states, but especially in the common law jurisdiction of Cameroon. There, among other roles, I have the privilege to work as a permanent visiting professor with doctoral candidates in law at the University of Buea.

Lawyers, judges and academics, whatever their preferred language, discuss technical aspects of the OHADA laws and the institutions. This book is an illustration of that reality. Praise of OHADA has been hard-won, and criticisms have been earned as well. Importantly, narrowly focused objections imply acceptance of the whole, and the negative comments in this book are as specific as they are professional.

With respect to OHADA's future in other common law jurisdictions, the most important point is that OHADA's neighbours will gain from the simple exercise of learning more about OHADA's laws and institutions, as that knowledge will facilitate cross-border trade. Thus, neighbouring common law professionals already now have reason to become familiar with OHADA. Ultimately, OHADA's neighbours may choose to negotiate terms for entry into a larger uniform system in order to obtain maximum benefit from the laws' and institutions' quality and transnational application. Legal professionals will have to demonstrate the advantages to the larger public, including current and potential clients, in order to create the political will to effect any enlargement. My guess is that law students and new lawyers will be the next norm entrepreneurs, because their future depends on OHADA's success and on the resultant economic benefits.

Claire Moore Dickerson
Tulane University Law School, New Orleans, Louisiana, USA

1

Community Laws in International Business Transactions

The late Professor John Ademola Yakubu, PhD
Professor of Law, University of Ibadan, Ibadan, Nigeria

Edited posthumously by Claire Moore Dickerson

OHADA, the acronym for the name in French for the Organization for Harmonization in Africa of Business Law, was formed by a treaty in 1993. The original parties were Benin, Burkina Faso, Central African Republic, Chad, Cameroon, Comoros, Congo, Côte d'Ivoire, Equatorial Guinea, Gabon, Mali, Niger, Senegal and Togo; Guinea and Guinea-Bissau joined thereafter, and as this book goes to press the Democratic Republic of Congo's parliament has adoption under review. An articulated purpose for the treaty was to provide the State parties with a modern, western style set of business laws and, thus, to make these State parties more attractive to foreign investors from the developed world.

Currently, there are eight OHADA statutes, and a ninth is anticipated in 2009. Because the treaty limits OHADA's jurisdiction to business matters,[1] these statutes, called Uniform Acts, focus exclusively on business matters. As Chapters 3 and 4 describe, these Uniform Acts govern the formation, operation and dissolution of business entities and the formation, performance and enforcement of business transactions.

---

[1] OHADA Treaty, Arts. 1 & 2, available at www.ohada.com. An English translation of the treaty is also at Appendix 2.

In addition to the Uniform Acts, OHADA creates four principal supranational institutions. As Chapters 3 through 5 explain in more detail, the Council of Ministers is the organization's legislature, the CCJA (Common Court of Justice and Arbitrage) is the supranational court of final appeal for all issues under the OHADA laws, the Permanent Secretariat is the executive, and a regional school is devoted to training judges and lawyers in and informing them about the OHADA system. The Uniform Acts, importantly, become the internal law of each State party as soon as they come into force through action by the Council of Ministers. The CCJA's role in this connection is to ensure that these texts are interpreted uniformly across the entire OHADA territory.

In addition, proposed revisions of the OHADA Treaty, circulating among the State parties for completion of the ratification process as this book goes to press, would add a Conference of Heads of State and of Government.[1] The delineation of jurisdictions among the existing OHADA institutions and this Conference remains to be worked out. The purpose of these revisions appears to include having the new Conference serve as the forum where State parties can discuss their national political concerns relating to OHADA. Until the revisions complete the adoption procedures, the current OHADA Treaty remains in effect.

The original State parties adopted the OHADA Treaty at a time of considerable economic dislocation. The more recent adherents saw the advantage of the OHADA laws' modernity and uniformity. Further adherents, for example from among the anglophone nations of Africa, will depend on those countries' internal political and economic assessments of the value of the OHADA regime. The analysis in the following chapters is designed to offer two perspectives on OHADA. The first perspective is from inside the anglophone region of OHADA, namely anglophone Cameroon; and the second is from an economically powerful neighbour of the OHADA territory, Nigeria. The goal of the writings that follow is to provide information about OHADA that readers can use to assess what their own country and its business people could gain from participation in this project.

OHADA is part of a larger movement to create commercial communities on the African continent. Recent efforts at sub-regional and regional levels have created bodies such as the ECOWAS (Economic Community of West African States), the EAC (East African Community), the SADC (South African Development Community) and the AET (African Economic Treaty), not to speak of the African Union. Each of these organizations

[1] An English translation of the treaty revisions circulating for ratification is at Appendix 3.

has its own goals; while OHADA's geographic territory overlaps those of the other communities, OHADA's sole purpose is to establish the legal structures that increase the predictability of commercial transactions.

The Way Out

In a typical case of a trans-border transaction, three conventional issues may be involved: 1) choice of law; 2) choice of the appropriate court to assume jurisdiction; 3) timely recognition and enforcement of judgements.

Issues concerning choice of law or forum, or concerning enforcement, increase the unpredictability of commercial transactions in three ways. If the parties neglect to agree expressly on the law or to accept jurisdiction, the indeterminacy of the application of conflicts of laws and jurisdictional principles intervenes. If the parties do specify choice of law and submit to jurisdiction, at least one party, and both if a neutral jurisdiction is selected, will still have to operate in a foreign law and jurisdiction. Because even the most skilled foreign jurist cannot appreciate the nuances of a legal system as clearly as does the local jurist, the foreigner's uncertainty increases the client's transaction costs.[1] These costs include out-of-pocket expenses such as legal fees for local counsel, but the cost of uncertainty as well. The party for whom the law or jurisdiction is foreign will be unable to quantify the risk as fully as would a local business person and, therefore, will have to charge more.

Community laws and institutions can provide at least a partial solution. If both parties belong to the same community, the community's law is local to both. If the community is one in reality, both parties will be familiar with applicable social as well as legal norms, including those relating to resolution of disputes. The promise of a unified legal system is that all economic operators within the territory will be using their own internal law and judicial institutions.

Community Laws: Approaches

Without necessarily discussing the historical antecedents that gave rise to the concept of community law, it can be said that community law

---

[1] Konrad Zweigert opined that 'the judge applying foreign law is a dilettante, a beginner; he is timid. The judge applying the lex fori is a learned expert; he is a sovereign, superior judge. ...[T]he judicial process has a lower quality where the judge applies foreign law than where he applies lex fori'. Zweigert, K. (1973) *Some Reflections on the Sociological Dimensions of Private International Law or What is Justice in the Conflict of Laws,* University of Colorado Law Review 44:283-299, p 293.

concerning the definition of relationships and the resolution of conflicts, especially with respect to business transactions, falls substantially into two categories: unification and harmonization.

Unification

This approach, as the name suggests, requires at least one of the participating countries, and perhaps all of them, to substitute a new law in order to achieve identity. Various nations with the attendant independence and power to make laws (sovereign power) mean various national laws as long as the countries concerned can lay claim to sovereignty. However, nations may come together for the purpose of having uniform laws to govern germane issues or particular transactions. Where community laws relating to this cooperation or agreement govern those issues, these community laws are substituted for the segmental or national laws. This unification effort will therefore produce uniform laws.

Harmonization

Harmonization relates to a process whereby national laws are not totally ignored, but instead community law becomes integrated within the framework of national laws. By community agreement, some degree of uniformity is achieved with respect to transactions that the community laws are to govern. Thus, national laws operate as long as those laws are not inconsistent with the community laws' requirements. Further, where national law differs in substance from the community law, the former adopts adjustments and amendments imposed for the purpose of achieving the objectives of community laws. Identity of the laws is not required.

Harmonization can be obtained by having a new set of laws replace the countries' existing laws, but it can also result from non-identical national laws that achieve substantially the same outcomes. The issue, of course, is that each member nation, and ultimately the collection of member nations, must compare and coordinate laws that are different on their face, and then agree on their actual impact.

In addition to a potential harmonization among the member countries, if the community has supranational institutions, these may promulgate laws as well, resulting in a need for vertical harmonization. In this arrangement, the member nations' local laws may coexist with the supranational pronouncements, thereby creating another area of potential conflict.

Federico Mancini, then Advocate General of the European Court of Justice, was keenly aware of the distinction between unification and harmonization. As early as 1988, he suggested that the European Community's member states were themselves leaning towards favouring supranational solutions facilitated by the European Court of Justice's decisions. As these supranational solutions become integrated into and not merely coordinated with national regimes, laws are increasingly uniform, both horizontally and vertically.[1]

Advantages to Community Grappling with Problems of International Business Transactions

Unification, and to a lesser degree harmonization, reduce transaction costs. The parties' familiarity with the system increases predictability in business transactions. The substitution mandated by unification has significant initial costs, of course, but the European Union, for example, is functioning effectively with a combination of substitution and harmonization. Within the European Union, there is a fundamental tension between the principles of subsidiarity on one hand and on the other, the concepts of direct applicability and direct effect concerning community norms, and of supremacy of community laws over national laws.[2] To resolve this conflict, community law has chosen to be flexible in approach. Regulations, which tend to be technical, are directly applicable irrespective of the contradictory state laws, while directives harmonize law as they are typically implemented through state-level legislation or regulation.

The European experience with harmonization suggests that harmonization can be less politically costly than unification. Nevertheless, all those who live in federalized forms of government experience the cost of redundancies and of jurisdictional feuds between vertical strata of government. In contrast, the OHADA State parties resolved the tension differently. They shouldered early the political cost of unification, and thus they have been able to create a large, internally consistent legal market more quickly and with less long-term administrative follow-up, than is the case for Europe. Indeed, within a very few years after the signing of the OHADA Treaty, the 16 State parties had established a

[1] See, eg, Bonell, M. J. (1990) International uniform law in practice – or where the real trouble begins, *American Journal of Comparative Law* 38:865–888, pp 868–69.

[2] Berman, G. (1994) Taking subsidiarity seriously: federalism in the European community and the United States, *Columbia Law Review* 94:331–456, p 348.

sophisticated and uniform collection of business laws, together with institutions designed to promote transparency and, more generally, predictability.

What, then, are the obstacles to OHADA's continued expansion? They include lack of political will resulting in the judicial and commercial infrastructures' instability and continued lack of sophistication and strength. Other impediments include the divergence of legal, cultural and social traditions, differing economic philosophies on specific topics such as priorities in bankruptcy, and, very generally, the continuing influence of the nations' colonial past.

After an introduction to OHADA, the chapters that follow describe the route that Cameroon took on its way to joining OHADA. They analyse how this partly anglophone country, with its mixed legal tradition, has experienced OHADA. They suggest how its commercially powerful neighbour, Nigeria, would fare were it to adopt the OHADA Treaty.

The authors hope that you will find the excursion both interesting and informative.

2

The History of the Harmonization of Laws in Africa

Jean Alain Penda Matipé

There are two options available to realize the integration of laws among states: *harmonization* or *unification*. Harmonization consists of modifying existing laws to attain substantial congruence among them and includes the coordination and coexistence discussed in Chapter 1. Unification of laws is more comprehensive than harmonization: it entails the elimination of any differences within national laws by the substitution of a uniform act for the member states' national laws. Because the OHADA (Organization for Harmonization in Africa of Business Law) laws are immediately and directly applicable within each member state without any additional implementation, although the OHADA Treaty's articulated objective is harmonization, it truly works towards unification.[1]

The first part considers the concept of unification in the context of pre-colonial Africa, where customary rules and the chief's word were law, or in the case of Islamic jurisdictions, where the Shari'a was the law. The Democratic Republic of Congo, the former Zaire, provides both examples of customary law and early forms of uniformization between existing laws and more modern ones. The Shari'a is its own version of unification.

In the second part, we will concentrate on colonial Africa. Here we will look at the applicable laws in African colonies and ascertain whether the colonial powers made any attempt to harmonize, either among the different African colonies or between the laws they transplanted to their

---

[1] Asssociation Henri Capitant, l'Organisation pour l'Harmonisation en Afrique du Droit des Affaires (OHADA), Petites Affiches La Loi, numéro spécial, le quotidien juridique, *Archives Commerciales de la France*, 205, p 61.

colonies and the existing customary laws. Pan-Africanism, with its aims and results, is an important part of this story. It also sets the stage for our future discussions by emphasizing the colonial experience of the one common law jurisdiction currently within the OHADA territory, the former West Region of the Cameroons.

Part three focuses on integration efforts today, their forms and processes, especially within the context of the AU (African Union) and its predecessor, the OAU (Organization of African Unity), but also through regional and specialized organizations. It thus situates OHADA's move towards legal integration within the other, similar movements on the African continent.

Legal Integration in Pre-colonial Africa

The term 'pre-colonial Africa' relates to that period of African history when the African continent had little or no contact with the outside world. European explorers, who had learned from the Americas, India, and Asia, had little or no understanding of the African continent, of its people, its vegetation and landscape. Indeed, they referred to Africa as the 'Dark Continent', and those very few Europeans who had any contact with African people readily described them as barbaric brutes, uncivilized and uncouth.

The African people did, however, have significant civilizations, and these had laws that governed their activities.[1] The laws were properly known as 'customary law': the indigenous legal rules, procedures, institutions and ideas. Similarly, Islamic law was and is still treated very much as African customary law, though its source is not indigenous tradition.[2] For instance, the Shari'a law or Islamic Law[3] is applicable in Kenya and in the northern states of Nigeria. To add complexity, various Islamic schools are represented in Kenya as it has a very diverse Muslim population due to Arab and South Asian settlement, local conversion, and intermarriage. There, Islamic law is applied by *Kadhis'* Courts, where 'all the parties profess the Muslim religion' in suits relating to 'questions of Muslim law relating to personal status, marriage, divorce or inheritance'. There are eight *Kadhis'* Courts in Kenya, presided over by a Chief *Kadhi* or a *Kadhi* appointed by the Judicial Services Commission. Appeals lie to the High Court, sitting with the Chief *Kadhi* or two other *Kadhis* as

[1] R. David in X. Blanc-Jouvan, "La résistance du droit africain à la modernisation". Paper presented at the Dakar conference, 5-9 July 1977, Revue Sénégalaise de droit (1977),33.

[2] ANA, Islamic Law in Africa, 215 (Oxford University Press April 1955 ed. 1955) at 156

[3] The Shari'a law is an injunction of the implementation of the Islamic law.

assessor(s).[1] Similar to the Kadhis' courts, other Muslim personal matters were governed by either Liwalis or Murdis courts.[2] These courts run separately with those over customary matters and are known as 'African courts'.

These nuances and complexities make harmonization, much less unification, difficult.

On a substantive note, Shari'a law and customary law both have their own notions of contract law, for instance. Customary law in the former Zaire maintained that an agreement or promise (contract) was sealed when the parties pierced with a nail a three-foot-tall figure known as Mavungu. It was the nail fetish. To break an agreement sealed by a nail was to incur sickness, trouble or even death.[3] In contrast, Shari'a had other means of creating an enforceable promise – and this topic is just the tip of the iceberg as both the Shari'a and the customary law also governed marriage and other personal relationships.

Legal historians have not concluded whether there existed any systematic effort to harmonize or unify laws in pre-colonial Africa, except as a by-product of conquest. Because Africans had religious respect for custom, and because the Shari'a is by definition religious, they were reluctant to fuse them with the laws of others, even for the purpose of achieving a goal such as unification of legal systems.

This analysis suggests that no consensual unification of customary laws ever took place. That does not mean, however, that no form of unification occurred as a practical matter. We know that whenever a migrating people like the Bali-Chamba and Bamouns of Cameroon wanted to settle in an area, they fought the autochthones. Three hypotheses can be advanced: the conqueror imposed its customs (law) upon the conquered, or it completely subsumed the conqueror's custom to that of the conquered people for the latter, or the result in the conquered territory was a mixture of cultures and law. The first is akin to involuntary unification; the second to rejection of any form of unification as two different systems would exist, one for the conqueror and another for the conquered; and the last, being an incomplete unification, is similar to involuntary harmonization. In the case of these migratory conquerors, the long-term outcome was a harmonization of the cultures of the conquerors and the conquered.

---

[1] The Constitution was adopted on 12 December 1963 and has been amended several times; most notably in 1964 when Kenya became a Republic and in 1991 when a multi-party system was restored. The Constitution does not provide for any official state religion. Article 66 (1) to (5) provides for the establishment of *Kadhis'* Courts.

[2] Hunton & Williams (2004), Customary and Islamic law & its development in Kenya, *Legalbrief Africa* [Online] www.legalbrief.co.za

[3] Encyclopedia of Africa (1992), vol. 2, Middleton, p 528.

Legal Integration in Colonial and Immediate Post-colonial Africa

The same type of harmonization proceeded during the colonial period, but on quite a different scale. True, the legal integration was imposed by the colonial powers, but factually it is the reason why there are broad swathes of harmonized laws, and even unified laws, across Africa.[1]

From about 1884 to the late 1950s, Africa was under the rule of European countries, primarily Belgium, Britain, France, Germany, Italy, Portugal and Spain. During this period, most of these European countries imposed their laws on their colonies. Britain, for example, applied the common law and equity.[2] But it allowed some customary practices to prevail, especially those that the British considered not 'repugnant' to their understanding of natural justice, good conscience and equity[3]. In British Cameroon, for example, Article 9 of the mandate on the Foreign Jurisdiction Act was applied, as Cameroon was a mandated territory[4].

An order-in-council in Great Britain is a decision issued by the sovereign on the advice of the Privy Council or few selected members thereof. As distinguished from statute, it does not require the sanction of parliament; it is issued by the sovereign by virtue of the royal prerogative. As used in this context, orders-in-council were extensively used by English administrators who act on the strength of the power conferred upon them by some act of parliament. They were largely used for regulating the details of local government and the affairs of the crown colonies.

The British order-in-council (No. 1621, June 1923) empowered Britain to rule Northern Cameroon as part of Eastern Nigeria. To rule its colonies, Britain used an administrative system known as *indirect rule* whereby traditional chiefs and their institutions were allowed to exercise narrow authority while serving as an intermediary for the British administration to implement its policies on the natives. The result was a two-tiered system: for British citizens and for issues the British considered to be central to their culture, the laws were unified under the British regime;

---

[1] Frimpong Oppong, R. (2007) Private international law in Africa: the past, present and future, *American Journal of Comparative Law*, p 685.

[2] In Cameroon, the application of English law is subject to Section 11 of the SCHCL (Southern Cameroons High Court law) 1958, providing for the application of English common law, the doctrine of equity and statutes of general application, which were in force in England on 1 January 1900.

[3] Customary law in English Cameroon is governed by Section 27(1) of the SCHCL 1955, providing for the recognition and enforcement of only customary law, which is not repugnant to natural justice, equity and good conscience or incompatible either directly or by implication, with any existing law.

[4] Bongfen, C-L. (1995) The road to the unitary state of Cameroon 1959-1972, *Paideuma*, 41, pp 17–25 [Online] http://lucy.ukc.ac.uk/Chilver/Paideuma/paideuma.html

for the natives, custom applied for certain topics, resulting in a form of harmonization to the extent that British law applied filtered through customary notions, and a much diminished harmonization for the topics that the British left to the chiefs.

France for her part administered her colonies under article 9 of the League of Nations Mandate.[1] In Cameroon, the applicable law treated Cameroon as the territory of an enemy state and permitted France to impose its military authority. The French then embarked on a 'civilizing mission' through her policy of assimilation, imposing direct rule instead of British-style *indirect rule*. The 'citoyen' was either a Frenchman or a native whom the French perceived to have evolved culturally sufficiently to be considered a French person. To both these persons *'la justice européenne'* was applied. A 'sujet' was a native who had not yet been assimilated; he or she was caught by *'la justice indigène'*. Theoretically, the latter was purely customary law, but in fact when the French reduced it to writing, they changed it to reflect their own jurisprudence, ignoring actual custom in the process. Traditional institutions, similarly, were at most tolerated.

Indeed, the French in colonial francophone Africa periodically made plans to record on paper the essence of local 'custom'. They sought to transpose the principle of custom into code-like lists of rules rendered, of course, in French. One notion that impelled some of this work was that ultimately, by comparing the customary laws of many peoples and abstracting their common features, a uniform code of customary law might be devised, one that would be simplified and somewhat tailored to fit the assimilationist aims of the colonial state. This project did not succeed due to the daunting task of fact-gathering, to its inherent internal contradictions which required paying attention to particular variations in order to produce standardization and to the difficulty of reducing active, nuanced processes into a simplified list of rules. Although most of the project ultimately fell of its own weight, the efforts at codification did modify pre-existing customary law without succeeding in eliminating it, thus resulting in a kind of harmonization.

To underscore the difference between the British and French concepts of unification or harmonization, consider the difference between the experience of Kenya under British rule with that of the France's colonies in West and Central Africa. In Kenya from at least the 1920s, but

[1] Article 9 awards the 'full powers of administration and legislation' as a result of the League of Nations' agreement with the French and British. The two powers were authorized to administer Cameroon in accordance with their laws and as an integral part of their territory, subject to such modifications as may be required by the local conditions.

especially in the 1940s and 1950s, administrators struggled with the question of how customary law could best be used in African courts. Prominent among their concerns was preserving what they saw as the fundamentally fluid and evolutionary nature of customary law. The British administrators sought to preserve these characteristics by rejecting the concept of codification. They asserted that reducing African custom to written law would 'crystalize' it, altering its essential nature. Custom thus was retained as a separate and only partially harmonized system, while the formal, 'higher' judicial tier was substantially unified. Consequently, the French far more than the British imposed on its colonies a top-to-bottom rough unification of laws, although a two-tier system existed in both colonial regimes.

Towards the late 1950s, Africans began to assert the need to take control of their own destiny. They started demanding independence from the colonial authorities. A possible contributory factor to this drive for independence was the Pan-African movement, which began during the colonial period, in the late 19th century.

Pan-Africanism's underlying aim was the unity of Africans culturally, socially, economically and politically. Pan-Africanism was concerned with the expression of Africans' feelings about their condition of helplessness and degradation. The seeds of this movement were sown as far back as 1881, by charismatic leaders like Dr Edward W Blyden,[1] who more than any other figure laid the foundation of West African nationalism and Pan-Africanism. He said that *'the African must advance by methods of his own… [w]e must show that we are able to go alone, to carve out our own way'*.[2] Subsequently, a series of congresses were held from 1900 to 1945 to foster African unity. Attending the latest congresses were the future leaders of post-independence Africa, including Nkrumah Kwame and Jomo Kenyatta. Upon return to their respective countries and filled with the desire to launch the transition from colonialism to self-rule, they became the champions for the cause of independence. Nkrumah's Ghana gained independence in 1957, and thereafter independent states held a number of congresses to discuss conceptions concerning development of political unity among these new African states. Harmonizing political

[1] (1832–1912), Americo-Liberian, educator, writer, diplomat and politician, he edited the Liberia Herald and wrote *A Voice from Bleeding Africa* (1856). He also served as the Liberian Ambassador to Britain and France and was the Liberian Secretary of State (1862–1864) and Minister of the Interior (1880–1882).

[2] This was recently cited by South Africa's then-President, Thabo Mbeki, at the work-in-progress review workshop of NEPAD (The New Partnership for Africa's Development), Johannesburg, 24 January 2002 [Online] http://www.au2002.gov.za/docs/speeches/mbeki020124.htm

ideologies of African states, not their legal systems, was an early form of attempted regional integration in Africa.

Disagreement in political and economic ideologies within the Pan-African movement led to the less politically ambitious OAU, formed in 1963, which later became the African Union.[1] This important but limited move towards integration did not focus on legal integration but is only part of the current picture: localized efforts at legal integration occurred immediately post-independence, flowing from the pre-existing partially harmonized colonial legal structures in the context of new political realities.

Legal Integration Today: Cameroon as Case Study

The Colonial Origins of Cameroon's Bilingual and Bijural Legal System

Cameroon, a Central African country, shares a border with four French-speaking countries (Chad, Central African Republic, Congo and Gabon), one Spanish-speaking country (Equatorial Guinea) and one English-speaking country (Nigeria). The territory was colonized by the Germans, who established German administration in 1884. This administration was interrupted after the First World War when the country was shared between two European victors of the war, France and England.

Four years after the end of the First World War, on July 22, 1922, the League of Nations conferred Cameroonian mandates on France and the United Kingdom. While the French mandate covered the majority of the former German possessions, the British mandate covered the remainder, adjacent to Nigeria. The French administered their mandate along with the French Equatorial African colonies. The British administered their mandate as two separate entities: Southern Cameroon as the Northern Region of Nigeria, while Northern Cameroon, after initially being administered as the Eastern Region of Nigeria, became in 1954 a quasi-

[1] The AU (African Union) is an organization consisting of 53 African states. Established in 2001, the AU was formed as a successor to the amalgamated AEC (African Economic Community) and the OAU (Organization of African Unity).

autonomous region of Nigeria, and finally in 1959 officially became part of the Federation of Nigeria.[1]

Immediately after the Second World War, on December 14, 1946, the French and British areas of Cameroon had become trusteeships of the United Nations. The following year, France terminated the trusteeship with the U.N., and formerly French Cameroon gained its independence on January 1, 1960. The future of Southern Cameroon continued to be debated, but what is clear is that up to that time, in political and administrative terms, the two British entities on one hand, and the French territory on the other, had evolved separately and had little in common with each other.[2]

Series of events progressed rapidly leading to a unitary state of Cameroon. Between late 1959 and early 1960, Northern and Southern Cameroonians were asked to choose between Nigeria and Cameroun. Plebiscites were conducted by the U.N.[3] As a result, Northern Cameroons, which before then had been administered separately within Nigeria, opted to join Nigeria and officially became its Sardauna Province. For its part, Southern Cameroons on October 1, 1961, became independent and joined French Cameroun to form the Federal Republic of Cameroon. While the former French Cameroun was renamed the State of East Cameroon, the former Southern Cameroons became the State of West Cameroon. The final step to create Cameroonian bijuralism was to fold the two states into a single, unitary country.[4]

The administrative and political separation of the former British and French colonies that comprised Cameroun did not last: on May 20, 1972, a referendum gave widespread endorsement to the proposal for unification. As a result, a majority of the voters had opted in favour of a unitary state. This state, first called the United Republic of Cameroon, has been known as the Republic of Cameroon since 1984. By this political evolution, the Cameroonians of today acquired their English-French bilingualism, and their dual heritage in the Common Law and the continental legal system.

---

[1] Bongfen, C-L. (1983) The origin of Southern Cameroon House of Chiefs, *The International Journal of African Historical Studies*, Boston University African Studies Center, 16 (4), p 657, and Bongfen, C-L. (1995) The road to the unitary state of Cameroon 1959-1972, *Paideuma*, 41, pp 17–25 [Online] http://lucy.ukc.ac.uk/Chilver/Paideuma/paideuma.html

[2] Bongfen, C-L. (1995) The Road to the Unitary State of Cameroon, 1959–1972, *Paideuma*, 41, pp 17–25 [Online] http://lucy.ukc.ac.uk/Chilver/Paideuma/paideuma.html

[3] Konings, P. and Nyamnjoh, F.B. (1997) The anglophone problem in Cameroon, *The Journal of Modern African Studies*, Cambridge University Press, Vol. 35 (2):207–229, p 210.

[4] Bongfen, C-L. (2001) *The Paradoxes of Self-Determination in the Cameroons under United Kingdom Administration: The Search for Identity, Well Being and Community*, University of Yaounde I, University press of America, p 132.

The English Cameroon Legal System and OHADA

In Chapters 4 and 5, we will be looking at OHADA uniform laws as they currently exist in a common law jurisdiction, the former West Region of the British Cameroons. As part of a general discussion of OHADA laws and structure, Chapter 6 will also analyse the OHADA laws' potential impact in a neighbouring common law jurisdiction and regional economic powerhouse, Nigeria. Thus, it is important to recognize in this historical chapter the British colonial legal history of Cameroon's anglophone region, the one common law jurisdiction within OHADA, and this also in the context of the general British move to harmonize laws within and among its colonies.

As we have seen, British *indirect rule* involved the use of local chiefs to implement colonial policies. The British authorities were the central administration and they appointed chiefs as native authorities. The native authority was autonomous in its management affairs; its primary obligation to the central administration was to collect taxes, in an amount determined by the administration, and then to manage the tax revenue for expenditure by the colonial administrators or on their advice. The fact that this same power was also conferred to some sub-chiefs threatened to unleash new struggles within the native administration as sub-chiefs saw the decision to give them also the power to tax as an act of political recognition[1].

Social harmony being indispensable to the British commercial control of its colonies, the British introduced the Native Court system. In Nigeria for instance, autochthones were superior authorities of the Native Court. In Northern and Southern Cameroon, a Divisional Officer (DO), had the final say over adjudication: his authority included reversing and modifying judgements. However, this position was not always held by an aboriginal, and as a result, the local people viewed these DOs as shadow presidents, known as "tafon", meaning the titular father of the chief. Although early on the local people respected the appointed autochthones for their personal character and their judicial authority, this respect was later eroded because courts were used not only to solve disputes but also to collect taxes.[2]

At that time, the colonizers had not yet formed the class of native intermediaries, the comprador class. Consequently, the colonizers sought

[1] Jua, N.B. (1995) Indirect Rule in Colonial and Post-Colonial Cameroon, *Paideuma*, 41:39–47 [Online] http://lucy.ukc.ac.uk/Chilver/Paideuma/paideuma-Indirec-2.ttml.

[2] Jua, N.B. (1995) Indirect Rule in Colonial and Post-Colonial Cameroon, *Paideuma*, 41:39–47 [Online] http://lucy.ukc.ac.uk/Chilver/Paideuma/paideuma-Indirec-2.ttml.

to replace the ineffective DOs by a new Native Authority System. The development and administration of this new system in the former West Region suffered, however, due to the inefficiency of its personnel, recruited among the local population, based on inherited title. Determined to improve the institutions, the colonizers unified the local government staff, seeking to place the new comprador class, the evolving educated class of aboriginals, and the entire Native Authority under a single administrative structure. Accepted theory in those days held that the natives will consent to effective colonization by other natives only if and to the extent that traditional power is respected by the colonizer. This perspective prompted the British to create a House of Chiefs in 1957 so as to provide the chiefs with a formal role in policy making. This power, however, was illusory as this body was not endowed with legislative powers.[1]

Upon careful analysis, the official documents creating the Native Authority and the Native Courts underscore that neither of these institutions reflected the true face of law and custom as it had existed before the colonizers' arrival. More generally, assumptions concerning politics of societies, customary law and land tenure, deeply embedded in these colonial institutions, were far from conforming to the reality of the pre-colonial period. These institutions were wholly inconsistent with the call for culturally sensitive colonial structures.

The perceived complicity of the DOs and, subsequently, the compradors with the colonizers' taxation regimes having rendered them ineffectual, the colonizers had high hopes for a newly educated class that the colonizers selected for merit instead of by inheritance. The implementation of education was thus of utmost importance to the colonizers, and in Cameroon it permitted the emergence of a new educated class of Cameroonian. Nevertheless, the education provided by the colonizers was replete with their fabricated version of tradition: the newly educated class could be dangerous to the colonization project unless it could be effectively co-opted. The colonialists allowed this class to rise very high in order to facilitate exploitation, not rebellion, and the class thus had to receive at least some of the authority that it had come to expect.

This effort on the part of the British was also a clear form of broad harmonization in the sense that the educated with any degree of authority would be practicing and implementing the culture, customs and socialization of the British system, garnered during their education. The trick

---

[1] Bongfen, C-L. (1983) The origin of Southern Cameroon House of Chiefs, *The International Journal of African Historical Studies*, Boston University African Studies Center, 16 (4):653–673, p 658, and Bongfen, C-L. (1995) The road to the Unitary State of Cameroon 1959–1972, *Paideuma*, 41:17–25, found at http://lucy.ukc.ac.uk/Chilver/Paideuma/paideuma.html.

here was that this fabricated version of tradition, very convenient to the colonizers, would be easily trusted and thus easily assimilated because the authorities implementing it were themselves native Cameroonians.

While the colonizers were extending education throughout the territory for instrumental reasons, the comprador elevated to the educated class struggled to emerge, mainly by emulating their masters' lives. In fact, this use of co-option of the Native Authority further consolidated the British social influence within the future elite of the anglophone region of Cameroon, and very specifically further embedded British culture, including the British legal system, within the territory. Cameroon thus experienced, through the pseudo-traditional, Native Authority and native courts, the British efforts at harmonization.

Meantime, agitations for independence elsewhere had not gone unnoticed in this territory, and the specific status of this territory as a UN trust territory made it incumbent on Britain to prepare it for independence.

Harmonization Today

Today, the harmonization of laws has become a central issue in Africa. A good example is OHADA. However, we must understand that this idea of harmonization as it is today stems from, or rather, is related to the objectives of Pan-Africanism, of the OAU (now the AU) and other organizations designed to foster integration. OHADA's creation was greatly facilitated by its region's legal history of imposed harmonization. OHADA's acceptance by its anglophone neighbours is likewise made easier given that business laws of Great Britain's former colonies share broad similarities. If the African continent's history contributes to the African states' ability to harmonize their laws, the current moves towards modern cross-border legal systems have a different source. All these systems, including OHADA, are part of a much larger, continent-wide, decades-long, thoroughly endogenous pursuit of greater integration.

In the general context of the push towards independence, the African states signed on 25 May 1963 the Charter of the OAU. Their priorities were to form a unified Africa, to defend the new countries' sovereignty and to further their decolonization and their economic and social development. The OAU summit in Lagos in 1980 focused on economic Pan-Africanism with the adoption of the Lagos Plan of Action and Final Act of Lagos of April 1980. At that summit, emphasis was laid not only on the acceleration of economic integration through cooperation but also on the deliberate promotion of national self-reliance, and acceleration of internally located and relatively autonomous growth and diversification. These goals were strengthened during the 27th OAU summit in Abuja, 1991. The representatives of the heads of state set out detailed stages for economic integration, first at the level of the existing regional regrouping and later at the continental level. These efforts, importantly, meant reducing barriers to free trade amongst member states, including the development of a common currency. The target date for the effective creation of the AEC (African Economic Community) was set at 2025. Regional groupings such as ECOWAS (Economic Community of West African States), and the IGA (Inter-governmental Authority), too, have worked towards this goal of economic integration.

Since the signing of the OAU charter at Addis Ababa, much time has passed. The OAU did not live up to early expectations, especially in the economic sphere. The Pan-Africanism doctrine of Nkrumah, Nasser, Modibo Keita and Sekou Toure ceased.[1] In September 1999, Muammar Qaddafi convened heads of state in Sirte, Libya, to chart a new future for Africa. At the end of this meeting, the heads of state ratified the Sirte declaration whose aim was to establish an African Union (AU). In July 2000, the AU was ratified in Togo, and on 26 May 2001, it entered into force, replacing the OAU.

The AU's more modest expression of integration focuses on commerce, not on politics. The new objectives include the creation of a common market for the purpose of creating conditions favourable to economic and social development and, maybe down the road, again some political integration. Given the new prominence accorded the economic sphere, including commerce, it is logical that some countries would seize the moment to focus on their business laws; nevertheless, the updating process has been uneven across the continent.

Meantime, still in the commercial sphere, regional integration arrangements have flourished.[2] Through economic organizations such as CEMAC (Economic and Monetary Community of Central Africa, Central Africa), UEMOA (West African Economic and Monetary Union, West Africa)[3] and ECOWAS (Economic Community of West African States, West Africa), and specialized organizations[4] such as OAPI (African Intellectual Property

[1] NewAfrican July/August 2002, archived edition, OAU The Early Days of the OAU, Special feature [Online] http://www.africasia.com/newafrican/na.php?ID=33&back_month=7

[2] Economic Community of West African States (ECOWAS), Union Economique et Monetaire de l'Ouest African (UEMOA), Southern Africa Development Community (SADC), Common Market of Eastern and Southern Africa (COMESA).

[3] Members of CEMAC and UEMOA, together with Comoros, constitute all members of the African Union who also are members of the Franc Zone. Comoros has its own currency, the Comorian Franc.

[4] Such harmonization has taken place in narrow areas such as intellectual property; see, e.g. OAPI (Intellectual Property Organization) and insurance law.

Organization, West and Central Africa), CIPRES (Inter-African Conference on Social Welfare, West and Central Africa) and CIMA (Inter-African Conference on Insurance Markets, West and Central Africa), a steady stream of harmonized and even uniform laws have sprouted at the regional level.

OHADA is an example of truly unified laws, specifically business laws. Unification of business laws means that every business person and every business lawyer within OHADA's territory knows the business laws of every other member state. This reduces transaction costs and thus facilitates economic development. In addition, as the drafters themselves expressed, the fact that these unified laws are based on Western legal norms reassures potential foreign investors. As we will see in the subsequent chapters of this book analysing OHADA laws in greater detail, the professionals dealing with the OHADA laws recognize and appreciate the technical sophistication of the OHADA texts. The extent to which the laws have a direct and positive influence on local stability, and therefore on prosperity and peace, depends of course on the entire context. As we will see, the effectiveness of its laws' application in any nation will necessarily be affected by the political, economic and judicial realities in that nation, but whatever those realities, the fact that OHADA's move towards integration is consistent with OHADA's larger environment is an important predictor for its continuing success.

Thus, it is important that OHADA stems from a political will to strengthen the African economic reality by enacting a secure legal system for the conduct of business on the continent. The other integrating organizations have not ceased to exist nor are they working in isolation. On the contrary, the work of the AU and its predecessor, the OAU, has helped create the environment that made OHADA possible. These structures, and the regional and specialized organizations, are complementary to OHADA, even as experts on the continent work to resolve conflicts of overlapping jurisdictions.

OHADA comprises 16 African states (anticipated to grow to 17 in the near future) and, as we will see, it is today an effective, operating, unified legal system. It exists not only in the former French colonies but, importantly, also in a former British colony, the former West Region of the British Cameroons. This region offers the best evidence of how other anglophone regions, having adopted the common law legal regime, would understand OHADA, the law of their neighbours, and thus benefit from the law's uniformity across their region. It also hints at the questions that these common law jurisdictions can ask themselves as they consider the costs and the benefits of adopting the OHADA regime.

3

Harmonization of Business Laws in Africa – An Insight into the Laws, Issues, Problems and Prospects

Honourable Justice Mohammed Baba Idris
Hon. Judge of the Federal High Court, Edo State, Nigeria

Whilst advising clients on cross-border transactions, I encountered OHADA (Organization for Harmonization in Africa of Business Law). Having learned that it applies over an extended territory and covers many business law subjects, I recognized the need to learn more in order to represent my clients adequately. This chapter is an appreciation of OHADA as viewed by an English-speaking, common law trained, former practitioner.

On the 9th of September 1999, the Heads of State and Government of the Organization of African Unity issued what is popularly referred to as the 'Sirte Declaration', calling for the establishment of an African Union, with a view, among others, to accelerate the process of integration in the continent to enable it to play its rightful role in the global economy while addressing multifaceted socio-economic and political problems.

The member states of the African Union's predecessor, the OAU (Organization of African Unity), in their quest for unity and economic and social development, had taken various initiatives and made substantial progress in many areas which paved the way for the establishment of the AU. Noteworthy among these is the treaty establishing the AEC (African Economic Community), which came into existence in 1991. It is commonly known as the Abuja treaty and seeks to create the AEC through six stages, culminating in an African Common Market using the RECs (Regional Economic Communities) as building blocks. The treaty has been in operation since 1994. This treaty came into existence in realization of one of the objectives of African Union, which is to coordinate and harmonize the policies between the existing and future RECs for the gradual attainment of the objectives of the Union.

As described in Chapter 2, in furtherance of this push towards unity and development, on 17 September 1993, 14 member states of the African Union signed a treaty on the Harmonization of Business Law in Africa (OHADA). Two more African Union member states soon became part of OHADA, and a 17th state is poised to join.

The necessity for this treaty arose because international resource companies investing in Africa tend to view African legal regimes as a potential risk. Legal and judicial uncertainties can discourage international investors and weigh heavily on one of Africa's main structural problems: a lack of investment. OHADA is therefore an attempt to remedy this situation. OHADA was set up to improve legal security and predictability in order to foster international investment and trade and to promote socio-economic growth in Africa. The framework currently includes eight regulations given effect by Uniform Acts directly applicable in the OHADA member states.

The Treaty, and the Interpretation and Enforcement of the Uniform Acts

The Treaty on the Harmonization in Africa of Business Law was signed in Port Louis on 17 October 1993[1]. The member states agreed to harmonize their respective business laws and enter into an agreement for the following reasons, which are outlined in the recitals to the treaty:

- The determination to accomplish new progress on the road to African unity and to establish a feeling of trust in favour of the economies of the contracting states in a view to create a new centre of development in Africa.
- To reaffirm their commitment in favour of the establishment of an AEC.
- Having been convinced of the fact that their membership in the franc zone is an economic and monetary stability factor and constitutes a

[1] Available at www.ohada.com and in Appendix 2

major asset for the progressive realization of their economic integration and that this integration must be carried on in a larger African framework.

- Being mindful of the fact that the realization of those objectives demands an application in the contracting states of a business law which is simple, modern and adaptable.
- Being conscious of the fact that it is essential that the law be applied with diligence in such conditions so as to guarantee legal stability of economic activities and to favour the expansion of the latter and to encourage investment.
- The desire to promote arbitration as an instrument to settle commercial disputes.
- The determination to participate in common new efforts to improve the training of judges and representatives of the law.

The treaty formed the Organization for the Harmonization in Africa of Business Law, sometimes referred to by its acronym in English, OHBLA but more commonly known by its French-based acronym, OHADA. This organization is charged with the responsibility of implementing the provisions of the treaty and ensuring that the objectives of the treaty are realized. It is expected to carry out these functions through the Council of Ministers and the CCJA (Common Court of Justice and Arbitration; Article 3). If fully ratified, the treaty-revisions signed in Quebec on October 17, 2008 will add a new institution, the Conference of Heads of State and of Government. This proposal acknowledges the national political implications of OHADA's supranational existence.

An overall majority of the Council of Ministers is required in order to lay down regulations for the implementation of the treaty (Article 4).

Objectives of the Treaty

The main objective of the treaty is to remedy the legal and judicial insecurity that prevails in contracting states by modernizing and harmonizing business law in member states.

In addition to restoring the legal and judicial security of economic activities in order to re-establish investor confidence and facilitate trade between contracting states, the treaty has the following objectives:

- putting at the disposal of each state, common rules that are simple and adapted to the economic situation;
- promoting arbitration as a speedy and discreet instrument for settling

commercial disputes;
- improving the training of judges and auxiliary officers of justice; and
- encouraging the setting up of an AEC.

OHADA's area of jurisdiction goes beyond the borders of the franc zone since by Article 52 of the treaty, membership of the Organization 'is open to all members of the African Union not signatory of the treaty', and to 'any other State not member of the African Union invited to adhere to it, upon unanimous agreement of all contracting States'.

Interpretation and enforcement of the Uniform Acts: Judicial process

Under the treaty, litigation regarding the implementation of the Uniform Acts is settled in the first instance within the courts and tribunals established by the member states, and on appeal to the CCJA established under the treaty (Article 13). The CCJA may be consulted by any member state or by the Council of Ministers of Justice and Finance on all questions on the interpretation and enforcement of the treaty (Article 14).

The CCJA is the court of final appeal and can hear appeals from decisions of the appellate courts of the member states on all business issues wherein questions pertaining to the application of the Uniform Acts and to the Regulations provided for in the treaty are raised. However, the court cannot make pronouncements on decisions regarding penal sanctions made by the appellate courts of member states (Article 14).

Appeals are brought to the CCJA either directly by one of the parties to the proceedings or by referral of a national court ruling on appeal, on a case to which it is referred and which raises questions concerning the application of the Uniform Acts.

Once an appeal has been brought before the court and the matter is being heard by the court, all proceedings in respect of that matter that is pending before a national court is automatically stayed. An appeal would not act as a stay of execution where the court declares that it lacks jurisdiction to hear the appeal in question. Where the jurisdiction of the court is challenged, the court shall reach a decision within 30 days.

Where any party to a proceeding before a national court raises an issue of jurisdiction and challenges the competence of the national court to hear an appeal in view of the powers of the court to hear appeals in respect of the same subject matter, an aggrieved party shall appeal against the decision of the national court within two months of its decision (Article 18).

Each party to the proceedings before the court is entitled to be represented by a qualified legal practitioner of his or her choice. The hearing shall be held in public.

Judgements delivered by the court are final and binding. Member states shall ensure the execution and enforcement of these judgements in their respective territories. No judgement that is contrary to that made by the court shall be lawfully executed and enforced in the territory of a member state.

Interpretation and enforcement of the Uniform Acts: Arbitration

By virtue of Article 21 of the treaty, in applying an arbitration clause or an out-of-court settlement, any party to a contract may refer an issue arising out of the contract to arbitration under Part IV of the treaty, either because the party is domiciled or ordinarily resident in one of the member states, or where the contract is enforceable either partially or entirely on the territory of one or more of the member states. The court does not settle such disagreements, but it shall name and confirm the arbitrator or arbitrators. The court shall be informed of the progress of the proceedings and it has the power to examine the arbitral decisions in accordance with the provisions of the treaty.

The parties to a dispute can agree to settle the dispute by a single arbitrator and may appoint that arbitrator by mutual agreement subject to the approval of the court. If there is any disagreement between the parties, the court shall appoint the arbitrator within 30 days from the date of notification from one party to the other to have recourse to arbitration (Article 22).

If the arbitration clause stipulates that three arbitrators are required to hear the dispute, each party shall appoint an arbitrator; such appointment is subject to the approval of the court. If any party refuses or for any reason cannot appoint an arbitrator, the court shall appoint one on behalf of that party. The third arbitrator shall be appointed by the court and he or she shall preside as chairman. The court may allow the choice of the third arbitrator to be made by the two arbitrators appointed by the disputing parties, and the appointment shall be made within a specified period of time. In such a case, the court will approve the appointment. Where the arbitrators are unable to appoint the third arbitrator within the time specified by the court, the third arbitrator shall be appointed by the court.

Where the arbitration clause does not specify the number of arbitrators required to settle the dispute, the court shall appoint a sole arbitrator unless it appears to the court that the case must be tried by three arbitrators. In such a case, each party shall have 15 days within which to appoint an arbitrator.

The arbitrators shall be chosen from the list of arbitrators established by the court. The list is updated annually, and members of the court cannot be listed.

Where there is a challenge on the suitability of any arbitrator to sit on a panel, the court may rule on the challenge. Where the court finds that the arbitrator is not suitable to sit on a panel, the arbitrator shall be replaced. An arbitrator shall also be replaced if deceased, unable to perform the duties or has resigned from office for any reason whatsoever, or where the court after an enquiry decides that the arbitrator has not fulfilled the obligations according to such rules of arbitration as may be applicable and as laid down in the treaty, or within such time as has been specified in relation to any matter.

Any national court of a member state hearing a case wherein the parties have agreed that the matter be resolved by arbitration shall decline jurisdiction, and where necessary, refer the matter to arbitration.

An arbitrator is required to submit each proposed decision to the court for review before signing the award, be it partial or final. The court may suggest formal amendments to such a decision.

Any award made in compliance with the treaty shall be final and conclusive and shall be a binding authority in the territory of each member state as if it were a judgement delivered by their national courts. Such decisions may be enforced and executed following an order for execution made by the CCJA.

Execution may not be ordered in the following cases:

- where the arbitrator's ruling is not pursuant to an agreement giving the arbitrator jurisdiction, or the arbitrator has ruled by virtue of a void or expired agreement;
- where the arbitrator has not ruled in compliance with the conferred mandate;
- when the principle of adversarial procedure has not been respected; and
- where the decision is contrary to international public order.

OHADA Institutions

Under the treaty as currently in force, OHADA comprises four institutions responsible for the formulation and implementation of the new uniform law.

The Council of Ministers of Justice and Finance

It adopts by unanimous vote 'Uniform Acts', which are directly applicable as part of the internal laws of the member states. It meets at least once a year upon notification from the chairman, such notification being issued on the chairman's initiative or on the initiative of a third of the contracting parties. The Chair of the Council is vested in turn in each contracting state for the duration of one year. A quorum is formed when at least two-thirds of the member states are represented at any deliberation, and decisions are reached by an overall majority of the contracting states present and voting.

The proposed treaty-revisions circulating for completion of the ratification process as this book goes to press would create another OHADA institution at the intersection of national politics and OHADA's supranational role, namely the Conference of Heads of State and of Government.

The Permanent Secretariat

This institution is responsible for the preparation of Uniform Acts in consultation with the governments of member states. It monitors and coordinates the activities of the Organization. It mainly prepares the annual business law harmonization programme and is responsible for the publication of OHADA's official gazette.

It has its headquarters in Younde, Cameroon. The Permanent Secretary is appointed by the Council of Ministers for a four-year term, renewable once. He or she is responsible for appointing his or her members of staff in accordance with the conditions for recruitment laid down by the Council of Ministers of Justice and Finance.

Regional Training Centre for Legal Officers (ERSUMA)

The school is attached to the Permanent Secretariat. It is responsible for the training and further training of judges and auxiliary officers of justice of member states in the new harmonized business law.

It has its headquarters in Port-Novo, Benin Republic. The school is headed by a director who is appointed by the Council of Ministers of Justice and Finance.

The CCJA

The court has seven judges elected for a period of seven years, eligible for re-election once, from among the nationals of the contracting states. The treaty revisions circulating for ratification as this book goes to press would increase the number of judges to nine, limit the judges to a single term, and allow the Council of Ministers to increase the size of the court yet further, provided that the need exists and the budget permits.

The court elects its president and two vice-presidents from among its members for a non-renewable period of three and a half years. The members of the court are elected by secret ballot by the Council of Ministers from a list of nominated candidates presented for this purpose by the member states. The court shall not consist of more than one national of the same member state.

The CCJA has the following attributes:

- It is consulted for its advisory opinion on draft Uniform Acts before their submission and final adoption by the Council of Ministers and also on the interpretation and application of Uniform Acts.
- It is the supreme court in respect of every dispute relating to the uniform laws. Matters may be referred directly to the court by one of the parties to proceedings before a national court or may be brought to it by referral from a national court. Matters relating to the Uniform Acts do not even have to go before the supreme court of member states.
- It organizes and supervises the proper functioning of arbitration proceedings; it appoints or confirms arbitrators; it is apprised of the progress of proceedings and examines draft awards, for which it may propose only procedural changes.

To qualify for election as a judge of the court, the nominated candidate must be from a member state and be:

- a judge who has acquired judicial experience of at least 15 years and who has exercised high judicial functions, or, under the treaty-revisions currently circulating for ratification, possesses the qualifications demanded for high judicial functions in the judge's country of citizenship;

- a barrister who is a member of the Bar in one of the member states and who has at least 15 years practice experience; or
- a law professor who has at least 15 years of professional experience.

Only two members of the CCJA may belong to the second and third categories; under the treaty-revisions circulating to complete the ratification process, one-third of the court would be required to come from these two categories.

The President of the CCJA shall appoint the chief registrar of the court on the advice of the court, from a list of nominees presented by the member states and who shall be of at least 15 years standing. The President shall appoint the other officers of the court, upon the advice of the chief registrar. Pursuant to the treaty-revisions in the ratification process as this book goes to press, the President would also a name a Secretary General to assist in the administration of the court's arbitral functions.

The headquarters of the court is in Abidjan, Cote d'Ivoire.

With regard to arbitration and to the functions of the CCJA, two rules of procedure have been adopted by the Council of Ministers. They are:

- the Rules of Arbitration of the Common Court of Justice & Arbitration; and
- the Rules of Procedure of the Common Court of Justice & Arbitration.

The Uniform Acts

Instruments to adopt the common rules are termed 'Uniform Acts'.[1] This Chapter 3 provides an overview of these Acts; for a discussion of how these texts function in an anglophone region with a common law legal tradition, see Chapters 4 and 5.

Preliminary draft Uniform Acts must be notified by the Permanent Secretariat to the governments of the contracting states which shall have 90 days from the date of reception to forward their written observations to the Permanent Secretariat (Treaty Article 7(1)).

The preliminary draft Uniform Act, together with the observations of the member states and a report by the Permanent Secretary is then forwarded to the CCJA which has to give its recommendation within 30 days. The final text is adopted by the Council of Ministers by unanimous

[1] Available at www.ohada.com.Translation into English of certain articles of the Uniform Acts, including all articles explicitly mentioned in the text of this book, can also be found at Appendix 4.

decision of the representatives of at least two-thirds of the member states present and voting.

Barring special provisions, Uniform Acts enter into force 90 days after their adoption by the Council of Ministers. They must be published in the official gazette of OHADA and also in the Official Gazette of each of the member states.

The Uniform Acts are directly applicable and obligatory in contracting states, notwithstanding any contrary provisions of a previous or subsequent internal law.

On 17 April 1997, the Council of Ministers adopted the first three Uniform Acts which came into force on 1 January 1998, following a waiver to the treaty. They are:

- Uniform Act Relating to General Commercial Law (General Commercial Code).
- Uniform Act Relating to Commercial Companies and Economic Interest Groups.
- Uniform Act Organizing Secured Transactions and Guaranties.

On 10 April 1998, the Council of Ministers adopted two Uniform Acts. They are:

- Uniform Act Organizing Simplified Recovery Procedures and Measures of Execution.
- Uniform Act Organizing Collective Proceedings for Clearing of Debts (Bankruptcy) which came into force on 1 January 1999.

On 11 June 1999, the Council of Ministers adopted a further Uniform Act, namely:

- Uniform Act on Arbitration.

On 23 and 24 March 2000, the Council of Ministers adopted another act known as:

- Uniform Act Organizing and Harmonizing Undertakings' Accounting Systems (Accounting).

And on 20, 21 and 23 March 2003, the Council adopted the most recent Uniform Act, namely:

- Uniform Act Relating to the Carriage of Goods by Road.

As this book goes to press, a Uniform Act on Cooperative Companies is being reviewed by the CCJA preparatory to being submitted to the Council of Ministers for adoption. In addition a draft Uniform Act on Contracts has been prepared and is being reviewed. Regulations on Labour Law and Consumer Sales Law are in discussion. Regulations are expected in the areas of Competition Law, Intellectual Property Law, Banking Law, Laws relating to unincorporated forms of business and the Law of Evidence. The Council of Ministers is unlikely to adopt any of these draft laws in the near future, other than the Uniform Act on Cooperative Companies.

Uniform Act: General Commercial Code

Before the adoption of the Uniform Act Relating to General Commercial Law by the Council of Ministers on 17 April 1997, trading was governed by very diverse rules both as to their sources (law, decrees, ordinances, etc.) and their object. The Uniform Act which is close to the economic reality and the life of companies should foster trade and make it safe between economic operators.

This Uniform Act, which contains 289 articles, comprises, in addition to final provisions, five books dealing respectively with:

- the status of trader (sometimes called a commercial operator);
- the trade and personal property credit register;
- the commercial lease and business;
- commercial intermediary; and
- commercial sale.

The scope of that Act is very wide as it applies to every trader, whether a natural or a corporate body, as well as to every economic interest group whose place of business or registered office is situated on the territory of one of the member states.

Status of the Trader

The Uniform Act adopts the classical Civil Law definition of trader (commercial operator) and of commercial transactions, while excluding from the list of commercial transactions contracts between 'dealers and traders'. In contrast, the list includes the exploitation of natural resources, the transactions of middlemen and telecommunication operators. It also contains provisions relating to the capacity of traders, the accounting obligations of the trader and the limitation of obligations resulting from commercial transactions.

Trade and Personal Property Credit Register

The Trade and Personal Property Credit Register is no longer a simple catalogue without legal impact; it receives the registration of natural persons and corporate bodies as well as entries of amendments and of movable securities.

In fact, there are three levels of registration: local registers kept by the registry of the competent court; national registers which centralize information from the various local registers at the national headquarters of the member state; and a regional register that centralizes information contained in each national card index, which is kept at the CCJA.

For most of the contracting states, the Uniform Act is potentially an important innovation as it contains provisions relating to the entry of movables.

Commercial lease

A commercial lease is any agreement, written or unwritten, between the owner of immovable property and any natural person or corporate body allowing the latter to carry on any commercial, industrial, handicraft or professional activity on the premises with the consent of the owner.

The Uniform Act regulates the obligations of the parties, such as the payment of rents, the conditions for maintenance and repairs of the leased premises, assignment and sub-lease of the property. It allows the parties the liberty to conclude a lease for a specified or an unspecified duration. The right to renew a lease is reserved only for the lessee who shows proof of having carried on the activity provided in the lease for a period of at least two years.

Business

A business comprises a series of resources that enables a trader to attract and maintain customers. It obligatorily includes customers and a sign or trade name and may include movable property (furniture, goods and equipment) and immovable property (right to a lease, operation licences and patents).

A business may be run directly or within the framework of a management lease contract. The manager under the lease has the status of a trader.

Commercial Intermediary

A commercial intermediary, who is a trader and may be a natural person or a corporate body, is a person who has the power to act or who intends to act, on a regular basis and as an occupation, on behalf of another person, called the principal, for the purpose of concluding a commercial sales contract with a third party.

The Act makes a distinction between three types of intermediaries in business:

- the commission agent, who is the person who undertakes in the agent's own name to carry out on behalf of the principal, the sale or purchase of goods, for a commission;
- the broker, whose habitual occupation is to put people in contact in order to facilitate, or to bring to the successful conclusion, conventions, deals, agreements or transactions between them; and
- the commercial agents, who are authorized agents whose occupation is to permanently negotiate and eventually conclude contracts of sale, purchase, hire or provision of services on behalf of and on the account of producers, industrialists, traders or other commercial agents, without being bound to them by a contract of employment.

The Act defines the role, powers, the legal impact or implications of transactions and the conditions of remuneration of commercial agents.

Commercial Sale

Provisions relating to commercial sale apply to contracts of sale of goods between traders, be they natural persons or corporate bodies. They do not apply to sales to consumers, sales after seizure, auction sales and to sales of chattels, negotiable instruments, currencies or foreign exchange.

The Uniform Act also provides for:

- rules governing the establishment of a contract of sale;
- the seller's obligations e.g. delivery, merchantability and guarantee;
- the buyer's obligations e.g. payment of price and taking delivery;
- penalties for the non-respect of the contractual obligations of the seller and the buyer, as well as exoneration from liability, effects of termination of contract and barring by limitation; and
- effects of contract e.g. transfer of risks and ownership.

The Uniform Act introduces the ownership reserve clause, that is, the possibility for the parties to postpone the transfer of ownership to the day of complete payment of the contract price.

Uniform Act: Commercial companies and economic interest groups (EIGs)

The Uniform Act is divided into one preliminary chapter which defines its scope of application and four parts dealing, respectively, with general provisions governing commercial companies, special provisions relating to each form of commercial company, penal provisions and final and transitory provisions.

Scope of the provisions of the Uniform Act
Every commercial company including those in which a state or a corporate body governed by public law is a partner, whose registered office is located on the territory of one of the member states, shall be subject to the provisions of this Uniform Act.

General provisions governing commercial companies
The first part comprises nine books dealing, respectively, with:

- the formation of a commercial company;
- the functioning of a commercial company;
- the civil liability of company executives;
- legal links between companies;
- the transformation of a commercial company;
- merger-scission and partial transfer of assets;
- the dissolution/liquidation of a commercial company;
- the nullity of a company and company acts; and
- formalities/publication.

This part contains important innovations, namely:

- A commercial company may be formed by a single person referred to as a 'sole proprietor' on the basis of a written document. A private limited company and a public limited company may therefore have a single shareholder.
- The registered office may not consist solely in a postal address but shall be localized by an address or a specific and adequate geographic location.
- The procedures for making a public call for capital are the subject of a separate title. Companies whose shares are listed on the stock exchange of a member state as well as companies which, in order to offer any type of shares to the public in a member state, resort to credit establishments or stock brokers or use any form of publicity or canvassing shall be deemed to be making a public call for capital.
- Auditors henceforth play an important role in the functioning of commercial companies. An auditor may ask for explanations from a manager who is to respond in respect of any matter likely to jeopardize

the continued operation of the company. When examining documents in the performance of the auditors' duties, an auditor may ask questions.

- The notion of consortium is acknowledged; control shall be presumed where a company holds more than half of the voting rights of another company either directly or by virtue of an agreement concluded with other partners of the company.

Special provisions relating to commercial companies

Any person, whatever the nationality, wishing to engage in a commercial activity in the form of a company in one of the contracting states shall choose one of the forms of company provided for by the Uniform Act. Chapter 4 notes the French terms used to describe these different forms. There is as yet no official translation into English of these terms; the English-language definitions below are thus at best approximations. With that caveat, the companies are:

Private Unlimited Company

A private unlimited company is a company in which all the partners are traders and have unlimited liability for the company's debts. The registered capital shall be broken down into shares of the same value.

Sleeping Partnership (Limited Partnership)

A sleeping partnership is a partnership in which one or more partners indefinitely and jointly and severally liable for the company's debts, referred to as 'active partners', coexist with one or more partners liable for the company's debts up to the limit of their shares, referred to as 'sleeping partners'. The capital is broken down into partnership shares.

Private Limited Liability Company

A private limited liability company is a company in which the partners are liable for the company's debts up to the limit of their contributions and their rights are represented by shares in the capital of a company. It may be formed by a natural person or a corporate body, or by two or more natural persons or corporate bodies. The minimum registered capital of a private limited company is 1 million CFA francs.

Public Limited Liability Company

A public limited liability company is a company, whether or not publicly traded, in which the liability of each shareholder for the debts of the company is limited to the amount of shares the shareholder has taken and the shareholder's rights are represented by shares. A public limited liability company may have from one to an unlimited number of shareholders. The minimum authorized capital of a public limited company is 10 million CFA francs, with shares of a face value of not less than 10,000 CFA francs.

Joint Venture

A joint venture shall be an entity whose partners agree not to register it on the Trade and Personal Property Credit Register and not to give it a corporate personality. The partners freely agree on the object, duration, conditions of functioning, rights of partners and termination of the joint venture, subject to there being no derogation from the mandatory rules of the provisions common to companies.

De facto Partnership

A de facto partnership shall exist where two or more natural persons or corporate bodies act as partners without having formed between themselves one of the companies described above.

Economic Interest Group

An economic interest group shall be one which has the exclusive object of putting in place for a specified duration all the means necessary to facilitate or develop the economic activity of its members and to improve or increase income from the said activity. It shall not by itself give rise to the realization or sharing of profits.

Penal Provisions relating to Commercial Companies

This part defines the various offences relating to the formation of companies, the management, administration and functioning of companies, general meetings, variation of the capital of public limited companies, the audit of companies, the dissolution and liquidation of companies and public calls for capital.

The Uniform Act does not deal with penalties to be imposed as they have to be determined by the various national legislations.

Final and Transitional Provisions

The provisions of the Uniform Act shall be applicable immediately for companies formed after the date of entry into force of the Uniform Act and within a period of two years for companies formed before this date and which have to harmonize their Articles of Association through amendments or by the adoption of new Articles of Association.

Uniform Act: Secured transactions and guaranties

This Uniform Act is an important amendment as well as a considerable revision of the provisions hitherto applicable in the member states which, with the exception of Senegal, had not amended the law on securities inherited from the Napoleonic Code of 1804.

This Act defines in a general manner the notion of security. It contains 151 articles which examine the following five distinct titles, namely, collateral securities, transferable guaranties, mortgages, the distribution and the classification of securities and lastly, final provisions.

Definitions

Article 1 of the Uniform Act defines securities as the means offered to a creditor by the law of each member state or by agreement between the parties to guarantee the execution of obligations, whatever their legal nature maybe.

Collateral security consists in an undertaking by one person to be answerable for the obligation of the principal debtor in event of the latter's default or at the first call of the beneficiary of the guaranty. (Article 2)

A secured debt consists of the right of a creditor to ask for payment, preferentially, from the proceeds of the sale of personalty or realty used to guarantee his or her debtor's obligation (Article 2).

Collateral securities

Surety bond

A surety bond is a contract in which the guarantor undertakes, and the creditor accepts, to perform the debtor's obligation if the latter fails to perform, possibly without the debtor's authority and even without the debtor's knowledge. All surety bonds are joint and several with the principal debtor unless otherwise stipulated by agreement or by an express legal provision. The commitments of the guarantor should be defined precisely (Article 4).

Letter of guaranty or counter-guaranty

A letter of guaranty is an agreement by which the guarantor undertakes to pay a fixed amount to the beneficiary on the latter's first call (Article 24).

A counter-guaranty letter is an agreement by which the counter-guarantor undertakes to pay a fixed amount to the guarantor on the latter's first call (Article 28).

Guaranty and counter-guaranty agreements must be recorded in writing and may not, under penalty of being declared void, be subscribed by natural persons.

Transferable guaranties

Possessory Lien
A possessory lien arises when a creditor in legitimate possession of the debtor's property retains it until he or she receives full payment of what is owed to him or her. This right can be exercised before any seizure, if the claim is unquestionable, liquid and due, and if there exists a link between the debt and the asset retained. The link is deemed established where the holding of the asset and the debt result from business dealings between the creditor and the debtor.

Pledge
A pledge is a contract in which personal property, tangible or intangible, is offered to the creditor or a third party agreed upon by the parties as security for the payment of a debt. A pledge may be constituted for past, future or possible debts, provided they are not voidable.

Pledging without dispossession
The following may be pledged without dispossessing the debtor:

- partnership rights and transferable securities,
- a business,
- professional equipment,
- motor vehicles, and
- stock of raw materials and merchandise.

General and special liens
General liens confer on the holder a preferential right on the assets of the debtor or on some of the assets only, for example:

- a lessor of a building has a lien over the furniture of the rented premises;
- a carrier by land has a lien over the transported property, on condition that there be a link between the property transported and the debt.

Real property securities: Mortgages
A mortgage confers on its holder a right of pursuit and a preferential right. A distinction is made between contractual mortgages, resulting from an agreement, and forcible mortgages which are granted by law or by a court ruling.

Distribution and classification of securities

The Uniform Act provides for separate classification for transferable securities and real property securities by listing the order in which they should be distributed.

Final provisions

Any security granted, established or created prior to this Uniform Act and in conformity with the laws then in force remains subject to that law until its extinguishment (Article 150).

By adapting to the existing economic structures and striving to clarify the applicable instruments, this Uniform Act is without doubt the one which brings in the highest number of modifications.

Uniform Act: Simplified recovery procedures and measures of execution

This Act sets out the legal proceedings that the creditor can rely upon to force the debtor to meet commitments (payment of a sum of money, obligation to deliver a good or to hand it back).

The text deals with two different procedures: simplified debt recovery and measures of execution of judgements. It institutes quick, inexpensive and efficient methods of debt collection such as the order to make payment (writ of execution issued by the judge against the debtor, in favour of the creditor) and the restitution procedure, which will be a strong protection for the unpaid creditor. Chapter 4 discusses this Act further, and Chapter 6 compares the Act with recovery mechanisms under Nigerian law.

Uniform Act: Collective proceedings for clearing of debts (bankruptcy)

This Act organizes the prevention of difficulties experienced by businesses and ensures the protection of sustainable businesses through preventive settlement procedures, especially intended for those businesses that have strong chances of financial recovery. A business in difficulty is entitled to make a settlement proposal which may be either approved or rejected by the competent jurisdiction. In the latter case, bankruptcy proceedings will ensue. The Act lays down a judicial recovery procedure in the case of insolvent debtors, and sets out rules with regard to corporate managers' responsibilities and obligations.

Uniform Act: Arbitration

This Act is framed on the UNCITRAL Model Arbitration law and applies to all arbitrations whose seat is located in one of the OHADA member states, whether the arbitration involves parties from an OHADA country or from a foreign state. The rules are modern and flexible. The purpose is to promote arbitrations as an efficient means to settle disputes. The Act is complemented by the Rules of Arbitration of the CCJA, which set out the functions of the court with regard to arbitration and other jurisdictional matters.

Uniform Act: Accounting

This Act sets out the types of accounting systems that must be put in place for external communication by persons carrying on business within member states. The law applies to the personal accounts of both natural and judicial persons who are citizens of member states. The Act also deals with the kind of information that should be contained in annual financial statements in order to ensure regularity and sincerity. It sets out the accounting system to be used in member states, and rules on the assessment and setting up of accounts. It deals with other subjects like the evidential value of documents, account gathering and publication of accounting information, amongst others. Chapter 4 further analyses this Act and discusses it in detail.

Uniform Act: Contracts for the carriage of goods by road

This Act applies to any contract for the transportation of goods by road when the place of taking over of the goods and the place designated for delivery, as specified in a given contract, are located within the territory of either an OHADA member state or two different states, one of which is a signatory to the OHADA Treaty. The Act applies regardless of the domicile and nationality of the parties to the contract of transportation.

This Act governs the various types of shipping agreements that can be executed within the OHADA zone and the shipping documents required in respect of these contracts. It deals with subjects like the liability of a carrier and other contentious matters.

The Act does not apply to contracts for the transportation of dangerous goods, funeral consignment or furniture removal, or to those transportations performed under any international postal convention. It is also inapplicable to those contracts for the international transportation of goods by road that had been executed before the entry into force of the Act. Such contracts shall remain governed by the legislation applicable at the time when they were concluded.

Practical Concerns

Financial Provisions

The resources of OHADA consist principally of annual contributions from the member states, loans concluded in conventions between the Organization and other nations or international organizations, and gifts and legacies. The conventions have to be approved by the Council of Ministers, while the gifts and legacies must be accepted by the Council of Ministers.

The arbitration charges shall be approved by the Council of Ministers. The annual budgets of the CCJA and of the Permanent Secretariat shall be approved by the Council of Ministers, and the accounts for each accounting period shall be certified by accountants appointed and approved by the Council of Ministers.

Status, Immunities and Privileges

The Organization has full international judicial capacity. It can enter into contracts, acquire furniture and real estate and transfer them. In addition, it can initiate legal proceedings and be a party in litigation.

In order for the organization to fulfil its duties properly, the Organization possesses on the territories of each member state immunities and privileges. The assets and possessions of the Organization are not subject to any judicial action, except where the Organization renounces its immunity. The Organization, its properties, possessions and revenue as well as those operations authorized under the treaty are exempt from all forms of taxes and custom duties. The employees of the Permanent Secretariat, the Regional Training Center for Legal Officials (ERSUMA) and the CCJA as well as the judges of the court and the arbitrators possess privileges and diplomatic immunities in the exercise of their official functions. The judges shall not be prosecuted for acts carried out outside their official capacities, without first obtaining the authorization of the court.

Language

A fundamental problem is one created by the provision of Article 42 of the OHADA Treaty, to the effect that French shall be the working language of the Organization. This topic is further discussed in Chapters 5 and 7, but this provision will create a problem for Nigeria. Certainly for anglophones, the single most important modification to the treaty contained in the treaty-revisions currently circulating for completion of the ratification process is that they increase the OHADA working languages to four: French, English, Spanish and Portuguese. If these revisions are fully adopted, the French text of the treaty and of the Uniform Acts will continue in full effect until official translations are available, and will control in the event of differences among the versions.

The related problem identified by legal practitioners, both in non-francophone countries party to the OHADA Treaty and those not, has been that of interpreting and understanding the OHADA legislations and jurisprudence which are in French. This topic is discussed at length in Chapter 5.

As a general matter, Nigeria as a nation is firmly dedicated to the promotion of Inter-African solidarity, regional economic cooperation and understanding, as its Constitution confirms. Furthermore, Nigeria's foreign policy objectives as stated in Chapter 11 of its Constitution, especially Section 19 of the said chapter, are geared, in part, towards promoting African Economic Integration and a just world economic order and also supporting African Unity.

The above provisions of the Constitution notwithstanding, the Nigerian Government would be very reluctant to adopt any treaty that excludes English as a working language. Similarly, the Nigerian National Assembly would be very slow to adopt any such treaty pursuant to the powers conferred upon it by Section 12 of the Constitution, to enable the laws to have effect as laws of the Federation of Nigeria.

Revision and Denunciation

The treaty may be amended or revised if a member state sends a written request to the Permanent Secretariat of the Organization requesting an amendment. The amendment or revision must be adopted in the same manner as the treaty. The treaty has no termination date, and in any case cannot be denounced during the first 10 years after it comes into effect.

Modification of OHADA thus is difficult. This is necessary to provide stability, but it does mean that even problems as basic as the identification of the working language take a long time to be corrected. As noted above and further discussed in Chapters 5 and 7, a treaty amendment in circulation as we go to press will add English, Spanish and Portuguese to French as working languages.

Conclusion

OHADA already has had a strategic impact on Africa's development, as it seeks to create a secure legal and judicial framework. Some of the benefits of OHADA have been to help foster improved economic development. The rules relating to several types of commercial contracts have been harmonized (commercial sales, commercial leases, security documents). Many aspects of civil procedure (arbitration law and enforcement measures) have been harmonized. The harmonization of legal rules has no doubt improved the reliability of the state court system in OHADA member countries.

Laws applicable to certain business transactions are now easily identified, and a common legal framework has been established within all the OHADA member states. The harmonization process will invariably limit the differences of treatment and encourage cross-border transactions. Conflicts of laws will be eliminated, or at least, limited. The process has undeniably created an accessible and comprehensive legal system, thereby encouraging international investment within the African sub-region.

Chapter 2 underscores that OHADA's harmonization of business laws is part of a distinguished tradition in Africa. The next two chapters illuminate the way forward for common law jurisdictions by analysing the experience of one such jurisdiction that is already part of the OHADA family.

4

Cameroon Offers a Contextual Approach to Understanding the OHADA Treaty and Uniform Acts

Martha Simo Tumnde, née Njikam, PhD
Associate Professor of Law and Dean, Faculty of Social and Management Sciences, University of Buea, Cameroon; Barrister and Solicitor of the Supreme Court of Cameroon

As discussed in Chapter 2, laws had been imported into Africa by the colonial powers. For all the harmonization imposed on the former colonies, the differing legal traditions created a fragmented legal environment which resulted in uncertainty, a multiplicity of laws and greater cost to investors. More urgently than ever, the challenges posed by globalization necessitate a push for regional integration of legal systems in Africa.

OHADA (Organization for Harmonization in Africa of Business Law), in contrast, unifies business law by having the Uniform Acts become directly an integral part of the national legislation of the member states without the necessity of any enactment by their national parliaments.[1] By

[1] As far back as 1963, during a meeting of the Ministers of Justice of francophone Africa, and also in 1991 at a conference of francophone Finance Ministers at Ouagadougou, Burkina Faso, seven legal practitioners under the Chairmanship of Senegalese-born Keba Mbaye set up to study the possibility of establishing an organization whose mission would be to ensure the gradual harmonization or unification of business laws in Africa. The outcome was the establishment of a treaty signed at Port Louis, Mauritius, on the 17 October 1993 called *l' Organisation pour l' Harmonisation en Afrique du Droit des Affaires* known by its French acronym OHADA. This treaty was signed by 14 countries and entered into force in September 1995 when the first 7 ratifications necessary to render it operational were assembled.

virtue of Article 10 of the OHADA Treaty, its Uniform Acts automatically and directly repeal all existing legislation, and supersede any future legislation, on the same subject matter.[1] It is beyond doubt that this reality has implications for countries acceding to the treaty.[2]

This chapter examines the institutional arrangements created by OHADA, and the nature and scope of the Uniform Acts, in the context of experience in Cameroon, the one OHADA jurisdiction with a common law tradition. This experience highlights some innovations and limitations inherent in the laws. As we will see, the success of OHADA will depend on the interpretation of its laws and the readiness of member states to amend, adapt and improve upon problematic areas of the law.

The OHADA Institutional Arrangement and Legal Framework

In pursuance of the objectives of predictability, transparency and security for business transactions, OHADA operates through four institutions[3]: first, the Council of Ministers; second, the CCJA (Common Court of Justice and Arbitration); third, the Permanent Secretariat; and fourth, the ERSUMA (Regional Training Centre for Legal Officers).

An amendment to the OHADA Treaty is currently circulating for completion of the ratification process; among other changes, it would formalize a fifth institution, the Conference of Heads of State and of Government. This new institution is a useful acknowledgement of the inevitable reality that any international arrangement, even one focused on commerce, has a political element. On the other hand, it may complicate already delicate relationships among persons and entities focused on commerce and be redundant since the political element is already represented in the Council of Ministers.

---

1 Cameroon ratified the treaty by Decree No. 96/177 of 5 September 1996, pursuant to Law No. 94/04 of 4 August 1994, authorizing the President of the Republic to do so and in conformity with a Constitutional provision. See Article 9(4) of the Constitution of 2 June 1972, and in particular, Article 45 of the 1996 Constitution, which provides that duly approved or ratified treaties and international agreements shall, following their publication, override national laws, provided the other party implements the said treaty or agreement. On this basis, the OHADA Uniform Acts are the applicable business laws in Cameroon.

2 For the benefits of harmonization of laws, see generally, Yakubu, A (1999) *Harmonisation of Laws in Africa,* Malthouse Press Ltd, Lagos, pp 27–42; see also Issa-Sayegh, J and Lohoues-Oble, J (2002) *Harmonisation du Droit des Affairs*, Juriscope, Poitiers.

3 See generally, Martor, B *et al* (2002) *Business Law in Africa*: *OHADA and the Harmonisation Process,* Kogan Page, London.

The Council of Ministers of Justice and Finance

This is the highest decision-making institution and the legislative body of the organization. It is made up of member states' Ministers of Justice and Finance and has the obligation to meet at least once a year. It is chaired in turn by each member state for a period of 1 year. This legislative body is assisted by the Permanent Secretariat, which by virtue of Article 6 of the treaty, '... prepares the Uniform Acts in consultation with the governments of the contracting states'. It examines and adapts the Uniform Acts upon recommendation of the CCJA. It is only after adoption by the Council of Ministers that a Uniform Act becomes part of the internal law of each contracting state. Article 10 of the treaty provides that, in matters within the jurisdiction of OHADA, national legislatures shall have power to legislate only to the extent not incompatible with OHADA.

State sovereignty is essentially a political notion that is expressed in a number of powers exercised by the state bodies, among which are legislative and judicial powers. One of the oft-expressed concerns relating to the OHADA Treaty is that member states have renounced their legislative and judicial sovereignty.[1] Renunciation of legislative power is evident from the following discussion on the law making process, but only as authorized by the OHADA Treaty, and only with respect to business laws. Consider that any state executing any treaty necessarily gives up some autonomy. The question is whether the benefits of uniformity outweigh the costs of constraints on sovereignty.

Articles 5 to 12 of the treaty lay down the procedure to be followed for drafting and adopting the Uniform Acts. Legislative power is exercised by the Council of Ministers, that is, by all the member states' Ministers of Justice and Finance acting as a body, instead of by the parliaments of each country. Pursuant to the OHADA Treaty, the OHADA Council of Ministers, in collaboration with the Permanent Secretariat, has adopted a law making process. As a matter of practice not specifically mandated by the treaty in its original form, the OHADA law making process allows for substantial national consultation and participation through the establishment of national commissions in each member state. The OHADA national commissions are comprised of representatives from the legal and judicial professions, from academia, the national parliament and relevant ministries.

---

[1] Kenfack, G.P. (1999) *L'Abandon de Souveraineté dans le Traité* OHADA, Penant, No.830, mai à août (1999), pp 125–134; Raynal, J-J. (2002) *Intégration et Souveraineté: Le Problème de la Constitutionalité du Traité OHADA*, Penant (2000), pp 5–22.

As a chronological matter, the OHADA Permanent Secretariat authorizes and supervises experts to prepare a draft law before it submits the draft law to member states for review and comment by their national commissions. Based on those comments and a subsequent advisory opinion from the CCJA, the OHADA Permanent Secretariat amends and finalizes draft legislation before sending it to the Council of Ministers.

The Council of Ministers of the 16 member states adopts the legislation. A proposed Uniform Act is adopted when at least two-thirds of the member states are represented and a unanimous vote is achieved. Consequently, each member state has the power to veto any proposed legislation by having its minister present and casting a negative vote in Council. This provision ensures general consensus of member states before any Uniform Act is passed and is designed to allay the fears of other African states that may wish to join the OHADA family.

Furthermore, it is evident that the competence and participatory capacity of national jurists and the business community who are members of the national commissions are a *sine qua non* for more effective and generally acceptable legislation. Indeed, nothing in the OHADA Treaty prevents national commissions from involving their national parliaments in deciding on the textual framing of a proposed Uniform Act. If the member states fully implement an inclusive approach for the national commissions, and perhaps even formalize them within the OHADA structure, this can help build and develop laws which are more congruent with socio-economic realities and the overall legal framework in member states. In its turn, this helps attenuate the bite of any arguments concerning loss of sovereignty.

The CCJA

The CCJA is based in Abidjan, Côte d'Ivoire. This supranational body ensures the uniform interpretation and application of the OHADA laws. It is composed of seven judges elected by the Council of Ministers for a term of seven years. According to the treaty, they are eligible for re-election once. In discussion is the possibility of increasing the CCJA so that each member state is represented by one judge, and that the CCJA is able to act in a timely fashion. Objections to this proposed increase include the fear that so large a body would be unwieldy and, as a matter of principle, the belief that judges should not represent specific nations. The treaty-revisions signed in Quebec October 17, 2008, and currently circulating to complete the ratification process, will increase the CCJA to only nine judges, whose terms are non-renewable.[1] The proposed revisions also authorize a further increase of the court if the Council of Ministers identifies a need and has the resources available.

The judges of the CCJA are elected from amongst nationals of contracting states, that is, judges, legal practitioners and law professors and the CCJA judges enjoy diplomatic immunity. Legal practitioners and law professors must have had at least 15 years of professional experience prior to appointment. Given that it is a court of law, only two members may belong to these non-judicial categories; under the proposed treaty-revisions one-third of the court must belong to these latter categories. The court elects its president and vice-president from among the sitting judges.

Jurisdiction of the CCJA

Articles 13–18 of the treaty grant the CCJA the following three areas of jurisdiction, the first two of which help ensure uniformity of judicial interpretation and the coherence and sophistication of the OHADA laws. As a practical matter, the third has served chiefly as a model for private arbitral systems within the OHADA territory.

These three jurisdictional areas are:

(*a*) Review, as a supranational court, of decisions rendered by High Courts and Courts of Appeal of member states in cases involving the application of the OHADA law.
This implies that it can be characterized as a *Cour de Cassation* having the unusual authority to render the final decision, or as a classic supreme court. According to the treaty, the CCJA's judgement is substituted for the supreme level of judicial review of each member state on any case relating to the OHADA laws. By virtue of Article 20 of the treaty, the decisions have the authority of a final judgement and are immediately enforceable in each member state. The CCJA therefore has the final and ultimate power as far as interpretation and application of the Uniform Acts are concerned, with the exception of judgements applying penalties.[2] Thus, once a judgement is rendered, it is *res judicata* and no counter ruling on the matter may be executed in the territory of a contracting state.
This does not, however, mean that the CCJA cannot be flexible. If it discovers that a prior decision creates significant hardship, it can reconsider and ultimately overrule its own prior decision. The case of *Les époux Karnib c/ Société Générale de Banques en Côte d'Ivoire*

[1] An English translation of these revisions is at Appendix 3.
[2] The area of criminal sanctions and penalties is governed by national laws of member states.

SGBC[1] demonstrates the CCJA exercising its flexibility. There, the CCJA first interpreted Article 32 of the Uniform Act on Simplified Recovery Procedures and Measures of Execution restrictively and confirmed the courts' inability to stay a forcible execution procedure, subject to the creditor's obligation to make the debtor whole if the creditor loses on appeal.[2] This decision met with stiff resistance from member states, such as Senegal, Côte d'Ivoire and Cameroon, because of the risk that the creditor would leave the jurisdiction without satisfying its obligation to indemnify the debtor, a result that would of course frustrate the appeal. In that case, the debtor would be irreparably harmed if, for example, the decision of the Court of First Instance was not properly motivated or the judge was biased and deliberately misinterpreted the law. Subsequently, however, the CCJA had the opportunity to revisit the *Karnib* issue in the case of *Société d'Exploitation Hôtelière et Immobilière du Cameroun dite SEHIC HOLLYWOOD S.A. c/ Société Générale de Banques au Cameroun dite SGBC*.[3] In this second case, the Court held that Article 32 of the Uniform Act has not abrogated national legislation authorizing stays of execution. In this way, the CCJA removed the hardship created by its prior decision. This is the sort of flexibility that is necessary to give effect to the aspirations of member states that the Uniform Acts reinforce the local commercial fabric.

Nevertheless, because the CCJA's decisions are final, it is here that the second aspect of the loss of sovereignty, that is, judicial sovereignty, is implicated. Undeniably, the supreme courts of member states are technically bypassed in OHADA matters when parties leapfrog from the Courts of Appeal to the CCJA. Indeed, the national supreme courts have not taken kindly to this. There now is evidence that at least some OHADA cases are taken to the national supreme courts, and that neither these courts nor the parties to the litigation are systematically referring such cases to the CCJA.[4]

(*b*) Consultation and advice on draft Uniform Acts that the Permanent Secretariat has submitted for comment.

The CCJA's second role is to provide its comments before the Council of Ministers can adopt the proposed Act. The national courts of member states, also, are allowed to seek the advisory opinion of the CCJA.

---

[1] Pourvoi No. 001/99/PC of 23 April 1999, Arrêt No. 002/2001 of 11 October 2001.
[2] See infra discussion of the Uniform Act on Simplified Recovery Procedures and Measures of Execution.
[3] Pourvoi No. 033/2002/PC of 4 July 2002, Arrêt No.012/2003 of 19 June 2003.
[4] See OHADA Treaty, arts. 14, 15 and 18 (concerning the authority of the CCJA).

(*c*) Administration and monitoring of arbitral proceedings before the arbitral centre, as contemplated by the OHADA Treaty's Articles 21–26.

Procedure Before the CCJA

The Internal Regulations of the CCJA which define the structure, competence and procedure were adopted on 18 April 1996 at N'Djamena, Chad. The court's procedure is based on written documentation; oral arguments are not required or, generally, expected. This preference for document-based proceedings applies to all aspects of the CCJA's responsibilities, including providing opinions to the Council of Ministers or member states.

Accordingly, any contracting state or the Council of Ministers requesting the opinion of the court must do so in writing, stating very clearly the matter on which the court's opinion is sought. Such a request must be supported by justifying documents. The Clerk of the court forwards the request to all member states for their views on the matter. This is done within prescribed time limits specified by the president of the court, after which the president fixes the date of the hearing and then the court rules on the matters submitted for its opinion.

The Permanent Secretariat

In accordance with Law No. 002/96/cm, a protocol agreement between OHADA and Cameroon was signed in Yaounde on the 30 July 1997, setting up the Permanent Secretariat of OHADA in Yaounde. The Permanent Secretariat is headed by the Permanent Secretary who, according to the treaty, has a 4-year term, renewable once. The Permanent Secretariat and its employees enjoy diplomatic immunity to ease the execution of its functions.

The Permanent Secretariat is in charge of the administration of OHADA and has a technical and coordinating role. It assists the Council of Ministers in most of its tasks and, pursuant to Article 6 of the treaty, it has the responsibility of preparing draft Uniform Acts in consultation with member states.

Where the Permanent Secretariat could have the most influence is in its preparation of the annual programme for the harmonization of business law, as provided in Article 11. It also has a duty to disseminate information about the OHADA laws, a contribution vital to their implementation. This is achieved through distribution of various publications, including the official gazette, decisions of the CCJA and of the Council of Ministers, and through execution of the Council of Ministers' directives concerning ERSUMA.

The Regional Training Centre for Legal Officers

Known by its French acronym, ERSUMA (*Ecole Régionale Supérieure de la Magistrature*), the Regional Training Centre is headed by a director appointed by the Council of Ministers for an unlimited term of office and is based in Porto Novo, Benin.

This school is in charge of training legal professionals from member states with respect to the OHADA Uniform Acts and those areas that are covered by the OHADA reform. The objectives of ERSUMA are fourfold: first, to ameliorate the legal environment among member states; second, to ensure the training of magistrates and other auxiliaries of the judiciary of member states in matters relating to the uniform business laws; third, to carry out research on African law in collaboration with the CCJA; and fourth, to accomplish all other missions conferred on it by the Council of Ministers.

Because OHADA cannot be effective if it is not used, and because it will not be used if legal professionals do not know it, the Regional Training Centre for Legal Officers is well placed to assist the Council of Ministers in ameliorating the legal environment among the member states. As OHADA contemplates expanding or at least becoming better known by legal professionals with a common law background, the curriculum of the programme could usefully include the teaching of comparative and African law.

The Nature and Scope of the Uniform Acts

Article 2 of the OHADA Treaty defines the scope of business law with a view to the law's harmonization within the member states. The definition covers the law relating to companies, the legal status of persons and entities engaged in commerce, the recovery of debts, as well as the law concerning secured interests, means of enforcement, administration of insolvent companies and court-ordered liquidation, arbitration, employment, accounting, transport and sales. This is not a closed list of subjects, given that the definition also covers any other matter that the Council of Ministers may unanimously decide to include within the field of business law, in accordance with the object and purpose of the treaty. By its decision of 23 March 2001, the Council of Ministers has expressly expanded that list (Decision No. 002/2001 CM), following a proposal by the Permanent Secretariat. As a result, the field of business law is now deemed to include also the law relating to banking, competition, intellectual property, cooperative and mutual societies, contract and evidence.

Since the treaty's ratification, eight Uniform Acts have been adopted: General Commercial Law, Commercial Companies and EIGs (Economic Interest Groups), Securities and Guaranties, Bankruptcy, Arbitration, Accounting, Simplified Recovery Procedures and Measures of Execution, and Contracts for the Carriage of Goods by Road. Currently under review at various stages of completion are draft Uniform Acts on contracts, consumer sales, employment and evidence; adoption of a new Uniform Act on cooperatives is anticipated for 2009. It appears that some of these new subjects may go beyond the domain of what is traditionally considered business law, although they are arguably both essential to business activity and likely to enhance the climate for investment. Because OHADA's mandate covers business laws, its reform already extends beyond traditional commercial law narrowly defined, and it will continue to expand as far as the member states choose to take the Article 2 concept of business laws.

By virtue of Article 10 of the treaty, the Uniform Acts are directly applicable and overriding in contracting states notwithstanding any conflicts that may arise regarding previous or subsequent enactment of municipal laws. This provision has given rise to certain problems of interpretation concerning the extent to which national laws are abrogated by the Uniform Acts. In CCJA Advisory Opinion No. 001/2001/EP of 30 April 2001, given at the request of Côte d'Ivoire, the court stated that the effect of Article 10 is to abrogate and prohibit any national legislative or regulatory provision which has the same purpose as the Uniform Acts and which conflicts with these. The advisory opinion also states that in cases where not all the provisions of a national law conflict with those of the Uniform Act, the non-conflicting provisions remain applicable.

The OHADA Uniform Acts deal with broad and general principles relating to business laws; the treaty allows the operation of national laws that do not conflict with the Acts. Thus, national laws continue to operate in any area not covered by the treaty's Article 2, as well as in areas expressly excluded, notably the imposition of criminal sanctions and penalties. The treaty also allows the operation of national specificities wherever the Acts' provisions are optional and not mandatory.

Nevertheless, the scope of the OHADA reforms and innovations introduced have caused much comment. The Uniform Acts are essentially based on civil law and have to a certain extent borrowed from modern

French business law. However, as we will see, there are substantial similarities between the common law and the OHADA laws, especially as to outcome but frequently as to approach as well. OHADA business laws are essentially a series of codified, market-friendly legal reforms which have also drawn many of their principles and rules from international practice. It is true that OHADA laws tend to favour a rule-based approach, as contrasted to the common law, which is more based on principles drawn from decided cases. However, even in common law countries, law is increasingly contained in statutes. In this way, OHADA represents a significant convergence of laws.[1]

Presentation of the Uniform Acts

General Commercial Law

This Uniform Act entered into force on 1 January 1998. The General Commercial Law is designed to provide certainty, transparency and predictability to persons engaging in commercial transactions. This Uniform Act contains miscellaneous sets of rules covering a number of subjects that appear oddly organized to the common law lawyer, but that do not fall within the scope of the other more narrowly focused Uniform Acts.

Book I of the General Commercial Law defines the status of commercial operators (*commerçants*) as all those engaged in commercial transactions and labels them as such. For purposes of the discussion in this Chapter, '*commerçant*' will be called 'commercial operator' because the other frequently used translation, 'trader', is too narrow to include persons involved in manufacture, transportation, banking and other non-trading activities.[2] Civil servants, judges, legal practitioners and other government officials are barred from participating in commercial transactions, as are criminals as well, thereby reducing the potential for corruption and fraud. The purpose is clear, but it is undeniable that, as a practical reality, government officials and legal professionals operating in the OHADA territory are often involved in business. The practical response consistent with the spirit but not the letter of the Uniform Act is to ensure that, despite the multiplication of distractions, the professionals are acquitting themselves satisfactorily of their primary responsibilities.

---

[1] See generally, Proceedings of the 4th International Conference on Law and the Economy: The Convergence of Law, 15–18 November 2005, Paris, France. Also see, the report of the International Law and Practice of the American Bar Association and the International Judicial Relations Committee of the United States Judicial Conference on OHADA Uniform Acts.

[2] General Commercial Code, art. 3.

Book II governs the operation of the commercial registry[1] whose purpose is to keep track of specified major transactions relating to business organizations and real property and to record security interests. The General Commercial Law provides for the establishment of centralized regional, national and local registries at provincial and divisional levels for the registration of commercial operators and of security interests in their property, which eases the determination of certain property interests. This is the most innovative provision of OHADA. However, it is worth noting that the registry provisions create neither an incentive for accurate record keeping by the regional, national and local entities nor any schedule of fees or source of funding to keep the registries operational.

Book III sets forth the provisions for leasing of real property in the commercial context, and for the sale of all of or an interest in the working assets of the business (*le fonds de commerce*). Book IV establishes specific, detailed rules for commercial intermediaries such as agents, brokers and holders of powers of attorney.[2] Book V sets forth the provisions governing commercial sale of goods.

Most of the requirements in these provisions are similar to the common law, at least in result if not in form, and provide security that may encourage local and international businesses to invest in the OHADA member states. Convergence of laws is strongly manifested; this is unsurprising as commercial law has long been the object of convergence. In the 17th and 18th centuries, two outstanding commercial lawyers, Chief Justice Holt and Lord Mansfield, worked to adapt the common law to the requirements of the merchants. They thus contributed to the eventual integration of the very international *lex mercatoria* into the common law.[3]

Commercial Companies and EIGs

This Uniform Act entered into force on 1 January 1998. It has 920 articles and is the largest of the OHADA Uniform Acts. It dramatically unifies

---

[1] It is known in French as RCCM (*Registre du Commerce et du Crédit Mobilier*) and sometimes translated as TPPCR (Trade and Personal Property Credit Register).

[2] This is an unusual power of attorney since it could be oral or written and it is not subject to any requirements as to form as provided under the common law system , where a power of attorney can only be created by a specialty deed. See section 117 of the Evidence Ordinance 1958; Fridman, G.H.L. (1990) *The Law of Agency*, 6th edn, Butterworths, London, pp 55–57.

[3] Lord Mansfield molded the diffuse collection of case law and rules on commercial disputes into a coherent body of commercial law, combining a mastery of the common law with a profound knowledge of foreign legal systems and a deep insight into the methods and usages of the mercantile world. He is rightly considered the founder of English commercial law. For the foundations of commercial law, see generally, Goode, R.M. (1985) *Commercial Law*, Penguin Books, Middlesex, pp 31–138; See also, David, R. (1980) *English Law and French Law: A Comparison in Substance, Tagore Law Lectures,* Sevens and Sons, London , pp 1–41.

what had hitherto been a confusing array of national laws governing partnerships and companies.[1] The first part of this Uniform Act covers general provisions such as the formation and functioning of companies. The second part deals with types of commercial companies, namely, the public limited liability company (*Société Anonyme*: S.A.), similar to a joint stock company under English law; and the private limited liability company (*Société à Responsabilité Limitée*: SARL) which is a more flexible form. It also includes yet more flexible enterprises and partnerships where at least some of the owners have unlimited liability,[2] namely, SNC (*Société en nom collectif*),[3] SCS (*Société en Commandite Simple*),[4] *Société en Participation*[5] and *Société de fait*.[6] Another interesting development, perhaps of considerable value to both foreign and domestic investors, is the provision for EIGs, which are formed for an economic purpose other than their own profits. The goal is to facilitate joint research and marketing efforts by creating a simple structure to share costs, among other possibilities.

The Uniform Act draws much of its inspiration from modern French company law and is better suited to contemporary commercial practices than the previous laws of member states. In this context, it is perhaps regrettable that the SAS (*Société par Actions Simplifiée*) recently introduced in French company law is not included. As its name indicates, it is a company subject to simplified procedures, whose advantages are inter alia freedom in drafting the articles of association, the replacement

---

1 See generally, Pougoué, P.G., Anoukaha, F. and Ngeubou, J. (1998) *Le Droit des Sociétés Commerciales et du Groupement d'Intérêt Economique OHADA*, Presses Universitaires d'Afrique, Yaoundé-Cameroun, pp 435–595; Nzalie, J.E. (2002) Reflecting on OHADA Law reform mission: Its impact on certain aspects of company law in anglophone Cameroon, *Annals of the University of Dschang*, 6, Special Number, pp 97–119.

2 These enterprises are called *Sociétés de personnes* and are based on the *intuitu personae* since the relationship is personal and what counts is the person himself or herself and not the amount of financial contribution.

3 This is like an ordinary partnership because each partner has unlimited liability for the debts of the partnership, although the SNC (*Société en nom collectif*), and not the partnership, can be formed only upon registration.

4 This is a limited partnership where there are two categories of partners: *active* and *sleeping* partners, known in French as '*Commandités*' and '*Commanditaires*', respectively. See Article 293 of the Uniform Act. The active partner has unlimited liability for the debts of the partnership and is responsible for its management. The sleeping partner merely contributes an agreed amount in exchange for ownership shares in the partnership but takes no part in the management, and his or her liability is limited to the amount of contribution made to the partnership.

5 This is a very flexible instrument where the partners agree that it will not be registered with the RCCM and will not have its own corporate personality. It is useful if individuals wish to form an undisclosed consortium or joint venture.

6 This is similar to de facto partnerships at common law where two or more individuals or corporate bodies act as if they were in partnership without having properly formed between themselves one of the types of companies or partnerships required by the Uniform Act. See the Fako High Court case of AWC *Njikam V Chief RN Namme,* Suit No. HCF/65/02-03.

of shareholders' meetings by written consultations or modern means of telecommunication and the absence of any requirement for the directors to give details of their remuneration in the annual reports.

The company law is in some respects more advanced and friendlier to foreign investors than the previous laws. The public and private limited liability companies can now have a single shareholder. The general principles encourage substantial disclosures to shareholders. This Uniform Act extends the notion of corporate personality to associations that hitherto had none, thereby making it easier for those companies to sue or be sued and to enter into contracts. The company law also governs liability for pre-incorporation contracts and provides for means of transferring the promoters' liability to the subsequently formed corporation and for release of the promoters. However, the characterization of the promoters as founders could confuse the common law lawyers since it gives the impression of continuous liability even if all steps have been taken to have the registered company accept responsibility for pre-formation and pre-registration obligations incurred by the 'founders'.

The company law has also clarified the position that third parties can rely on the apparent authority of the Board of Directors, or analogue for non-corporate forms, without the need to examine a company's purposes and constituent documents.

The formative document available to the public through the registry contains significant information, including the names of the first contributors to capital and of the first managers, and the location of the company's actual headquarters.

To the extent that the formative document is a contract among constituent groups, it prescribes rules for the governance of the corporation. The company law provisions prescribe detailed rules concerning the duties, responsibilities and powers of management, thereby limiting the operating flexibility of the company.[1] For companies over a specified size, special statutory auditors are required. These auditors have extensive roles: they are assigned a duty of both advice and control, and are to serve as independent guardians of management integrity.

Finally, the Uniform Act deals with the restructuring and transformation of companies and makes provisions for companies which make public offerings.[2] In the member states, public offerings are regulated not only by the Uniform Act but also by two other regional integration organizations, the UEMOA (*Union Economique et Monétaire Ouest Africaine*) and

[1] Articles 317–384 of the Uniform Act.
[2] Articles 81–96.

the CEMAC (*Communauté Economique et Monétaire de l'Afrique Centrale*).[1]

Secured Transactions and Guaranties

This Uniform Act on secured transactions entered into force on 1 January 1 1998. It governs security interests in personal and real property, or what a civil law–trained lawyer would recognize as movable and immovable property. The secured transactions law is divided into five parts. The first part on personal security interests deals with collateral security interests, for example with surety bonds and letters of guaranty. The second part, on securities in personal property, covers rights of retention, pledges, security interests without dispossession and liens on personal property. The third part, on mortgages, governs legal and equitable mortgages or interests in real property. It is clear that the customary practice of pledging land has been superseded by the mortgage provisions of the Uniform Act. This law makes a clear distinction between personalty and realty. It is worth noting that under this Uniform Act only movable and intangible property can be pledged and only immovable property, that is real property, can be mortgaged.

The fourth and fifth parts of the Act govern priorities, and the distribution of proceeds upon execution of the judgement, and interests in personal security interests, personal property and real property.

The Uniform Act on secured transactions is a coherent body of law, and many of its basic terms and concepts are similar to the common law and are also consistent with international business practice. This Uniform Act has the essential elements necessary to create a modern and efficient system of personal and real property securities. The law provides various guaranties which protect creditors, including banks, by securing the enforcement of their debtor's obligation.

However, the Act on secured transactions frequently leaves important issues to be decided by the national laws of member states. The result weakens the treaty's goal of uniformity of law among member states. This may compel potential lenders to research and monitor the laws of each state, thereby increasing the cost of lending. For example, Article 49(2) refers to the national law of evidence with respect to the existence of a pledge, and Article 122 refers to national laws governing the registration of mortgages. In Cameroon, the national law on obtaining a land certificate

[1] Two competing stock exchanges have been set up in these regions: The Cameroon Stock Exchange called the BCVM (*Bourse Camerounaise des Valeurs Mobilières*) based in Douala and the Central African Stock Exchange called the BVMAC (*Bourse des Valeurs Mobilières d'Afrique Centrale*) based in Libreville, Gabon.

and on the registration of pledges is very cumbersome and expensive. Unless the registration procedures are simplified, most pledges of personalty and many mortgages will not, as a practical matter, be registered since they often involve small amounts and are common in the rural areas.

Collective Procedures for the Clearing of Debts (Bankruptcy Law)

This Uniform Act entered into force on 1 January 1999. It provides three different types of collective procedures for the clearing of debts for both companies and individuals, namely, preventive settlement (*règlement préventif*), reorganization (*redressement judiciaire*) and liquidation (*liquidation judiciaire*).

The stay of enforcement of guarantor liability in Article 18 and the continuing liability as found in Articles 174 and 183 would act as an inducement for the managers of business entities to seek workable preventive settlements. The Bankruptcy Law provides that a significant amount of information must be delivered to creditors concerning the debtor's financial situation.[1]

However, it is worth noting the prescribed time periods for action by the courts, receivers, debtor and the creditors, are designed to further the goal that assets be returned to productive use as rapidly as possible. For example, under Article 7, the debtor has only 30 days to draw up a business plan to return the company to profitable operation. This appears to be a very short time to prepare a plan to reconstruct the business. Furthermore, there appears to be no provision to permit a court to grant extensions on these time periods if a court or other party cannot meet the time restrictions.

Arbitration

The Uniform Act on Arbitration entered into force on 11 June 1999. This Uniform Act provides a comprehensive system for giving effect to agreements that provide for arbitration in any of the member states. OHADA has created two different sets of legislation applicable to arbitration, as has been already briefly described in the introduction to the CCJA. It provides a unique and innovative structure for resolving disputes.

First, there is institutional arbitration supervised by the CCJA, in accordance with its internal regulations.

Second, there is the Uniform Act on Arbitration which lays down basic rules that can be applied to any arbitration where the seat of the arbitral

[1] Uniform Act on Collective Procedures for the Clearing of Debts, Arts. 6 & 7.

tribunal is in one of the member states, or that might also be chosen by the parties as the applicable procedural law even if the seat of the tribunal is not in a member state. As is the case of all Uniform Acts, this one is governed by the OHADA Treaty. The arbitral rules closely conform to international standards such as those of the ICC (International Chamber of Commerce) Rules of Arbitration.

The OHADA arbitration law requires courts to stay proceedings in favour of arbitration and provides standards for recognition of arbitral awards. It provides the principles and procedures for arbitration, including designation of the arbitrators, rendering of decisions and exequatur. Three forms of recourse are available, namely actions for cancellation, petition for review and opposition by a third party.

However, it would appear that certain provisions that may be very important to participants in international commercial arbitrations have been left out. The arbitration law could borrow from The UNCITRAL Model law on International Commercial Arbitration.

Accounting

This Uniform Act was adopted in Yaounde on 24 March 2000, and entered into force on the following dates: 1 January 2001 for companies' individual accounts and 1 January 2002 for consolidated and combined accounts. It lays down a harmonized accounting system for companies located in member states. It sets out comprehensive provisions concerning accounting standards, the obligation to present annual accounts, rules for the evaluation and determination of net income, auditing, publication of accounting information, consolidation of accounts and, subject to the member states' national judicial systems, criminal penalties. It is also worth mentioning that the accounting principles under OHADA are very similar to the international accounting standards. These OHADA provisions are a basis for the more detailed rules of the accounting profession.

The fundamental aim of these general accounting principles is to ensure the reliability, clarity and comparability of financial information and, more generally, its transparency and accuracy through significant disclosure requirements.[1]

The Uniform Act created two new sets of obligations. First, it established three different tiers of accounting obligations depending on the size of the company and second, it provided for the preparation of consolidated or combined accounts for groups of companies.

All companies operating in Cameroon are required to file tax return forms based on the OHADA accounting system with the Department of

[1] Uniform Act on Accounting, Arts. 8-10.

Taxation and the Department of Statistics. These forms (referred to as DSF or *Déclaration Statistique et Fiscale*) are the only financial statements prepared for delivery to stakeholders by most entities in Cameroon. There is an abridged version of the forms for medium-sized companies, whilst small entities file simple cash-basis financial statements in conformity with the OHADA Uniform Act. Some accountants claim that this arrangement appears to have enhanced the level of compliance with OHADA since it has alleviated the burden of excessive regulation on small businesses, which constitute a large proportion of reporting entities in Cameroon.

Although a high level of compliance was observed for small firms that file simple cash-basis accounts, a number of implementation bottlenecks were noted in the context of entities in the anglophone provinces that are required to prepare the full OHADA DSF report.[1] First, an authoritative English-language translation of the OHADA Uniform Act on Accounting is still lacking. Second, the quality of most translations that do exist for the Act leaves very much to be desired. For example, in all the cash flow statements (Table 7A of the DSF) '*Capacité d'autofinancement*' was erroneously translated as 'Global Self-financing Capacity' which is completely incomprehensible and misleading. (The correct translation of '*Capacité d'autofinancement*' is 'Cash flows from operations.') Third, the translation problem alluded to above is exacerbated by a lack of appreciation on the part of some anglophone accountants of the macroeconomic orientation of the OHADA accounting systems. For example, terms such as the 'value added' and 'intermediate consumption', and the rationale for including self-constructed assets and production in income statements will not be readily understood by an Anglo-Saxon accountant who is not conversant with the basic tenets of the 'by nature' approach to income measurement.

The above issues have serious implications for the education and training of accounting technicians who will be required to implement the OHADA model. For example, if official translations of the chart of accounts are extremely poor or non-existent, then examination questions (*Capacité* or *Baccalaure*) based on these pronouncements will also be of poor quality, thus devaluing the teaching and learning experience in English-speaking technical schools.

Furthermore, OHADA prescribes many accounting practices which are not compatible with IFRSs (International Financial Reporting Standards).

[1] See the Proceedings of the OHADA Accounting Seminar on the theme: *The Implementation of the OHADA Accounting System: Problems and Prospects*, 15–16 September 2005, University of Buea, Cameroon.

This in itself is not a criticism because international accounting standards were not specifically designed to meet the exigencies of small- and medium-sized companies that dominate the economies of developing nations. Nor are they necessarily appropriate for their environmental settings. Nonetheless, the World Bank requires all large corporations in developing countries to adopt IFRSs as part of its transparency and good governance strategy. Also, all foreign companies that are listed on European stock exchanges are required to adopt IFRSs.

Simplified Recovery Procedures and Measures of Execution

This Uniform Act entered into force on 10 April 1998. The Uniform Act effectively consolidates several different remedies for collecting debts and provides a framework for obtaining writs of execution on various types of property. The simplified procedures described in Book I provide for two types of orders, namely, the traditional *order to make payment* and the more innovative *order to deliver* or to return specific personal property. The simplified recovery procedure called order to make payment is virtually the same as the provisions in Cameroon before OHADA. This is also similar to the common law procedure under the undefended list action in many English-speaking countries,[1] as more fully discussed in Chapter 6.

OHADA also provides continuing opportunities for voluntary resolution or conciliation of disputes. Although the Uniform Act's provisions mandating attempts at conciliation may delay enforcement of debts in some circumstances, they encourage the parties to resolve their differences, and they may facilitate creative solutions for the payment of debts. The commitment to conciliation is one of the notable strengths of this law.

Under Measures of Execution in Book II, the law grants the creditor a large range of responses. It allows sequestration of assets, seizure for sale, seizure of debts, attachment and transfer of earnings, apprehension and seizure of assets, including special provisions relating to intangible partnership interests and securities, attachment of real property and additional provisions for the distribution of proceeds to creditors. The procedures described in the law are flexible. For example, under Article 130, additional creditors need not pursue numerous parallel proceedings; they can join the seizure operations of the first creditor by way of opposition. The law provides the procedures to seize the debtor's property and to sell it in satisfaction of the debt, including provisions for seizure of property in the hands of the debtor or in the hands of a third party. The

[1] See Order 3 Rule 9 of Cap 211 High Court Civil Procedure Rules 1948 (UK).

law also allows seized property to be sold at a private sale or by a public auctioneer. To balance the procedure, the law includes provisions for opposing the seizure and sale of property and for dispute-resolution procedures.

The implementation of this Uniform Act has been most problematic and it is the least understood of all the Uniform Acts in Cameroon. The problems may well result from the centrality of execution to the effectiveness of all commercial laws, and the inevitability under the OHADA regime of relying on national judicial systems whenever judgements are to be executed. Indeed, the importance of the measures of execution cannot be overemphasized since it is the final stage in a judicial process. The Uniform Act on Simplified Recovery Procedures and Measures of Execution is of general application and therefore supersedes all previous national legislation in this respect.

A particular problem of substantial practical significance arose in Cameroon concerning provisional execution of court judgements. There was a question whether prior law,[1] whereby provisional execution when ordered could be stayed by a superior court, is incompatible with Article 32 of the Uniform Act. Although Article 32 of the Uniform Act provides that except for immovable property, provisional execution cannot be stayed and the creditor can carry it through to its logical conclusion, the *SEHIC* case described above in the discussion of the CCJA's flexibility held that Article 32 of the Uniform Act has in fact not abrogated national legislation on stays of execution which, in that case, permitted the grant of a stay. By its decision, the CCJA balanced the interests of creditors and debtors: it used the full extent of its flexibility to recognize commercial reality and to thus help establish an environment appropriate for commercial transactions.

The provision concerning state immunity from forcible execution has also generated many problems in Cameroon. What happens if a litigant wins a labour suit against a state corporation? Outside of OHADA, of course, the state corporation will most likely try to brandish the immunity card, subject to any generally applicable exception to immunity for commercial transactions.

Article 30 of the Uniform Act addresses the issue and recognizes rights of the state, its agencies and public corporations to immunity from execution, to the extent the immunity is created outside the OHADA context. It also creates a right of a creditor to set off any liquidated obligation it may have in favour of the otherwise immune debtor, against

[1] Law No. 92/008 of 14 August 1992 as amended.

the liquidated obligations of that debtor in its own favour. This provision has been accorded extensive interpretation to include public establishments and enterprises and parastatals, and also relates to all acts and operations by these persons whether or not the activities are commercial.[1] If the judicial system is not capable of independently assessing whether the otherwise immune debtor's obligation has been liquidated, Article 30 means, as a practical matter, that unless and until a public company or a parastatal admits or acknowledges the debt or judgement, the set off, and therefore any execution on the debt is highly unlikely.

In most of the Uniform Acts reference is made either to the 'competent court' in the member state or to the 'president of the competent court'. For example, Article 49 of the Uniform Act on Simplified Recovery Procedures and Measures of Execution provides that the competent authority to rule on all disputes or petitions relating to a forced act of performance or sequestration shall be the president of the court ruling in urgent proceedings or the judge delegated by him or her.

In Cameroon, under the civil law system operating in the French-speaking provinces, practice establishes that this is the '*juge des référés*'. In the common law system operating in the English-speaking provinces, by way of contrast, urgent matters are entertained by the president of the court of first instance, or of the high court or of the court of appeal, depending on where the litigation is then located, subject to any delegation.[2] Other OHADA jurisdictions will have their own procedures, and the OHADA law is purposefully written flexibly to take these into account.

It will be important for each jurisdiction to assess the impact of Article 49 on its own procedure. Consider, for example, its impact in anglophone Cameroon. The mere fact that the procedures are different is not a problem from OHADA's perspective, whatever the issue may be under local Cameroonian conceptions of national unity. What may be an OHADA-relevant concern, however, is that because of the different legal traditions, the impacts may be different from one region of OHADA to another, a result at odds with OHADA's quest for uniformity.

Outcomes may be different because the judge to whom one region gives the authority to make urgent determinations may be less qualified for that purpose than a judge appointed according to the other region's system. Specifically, the notions of courts of execution and cases of difficulties of execution of court judgements have not been apprehended

[1] See Circular letter No. 041/CD/50.510/SG/MJ. of 6 June 2000 from the Ministry of Justice.

[2] See Article 2(2) (new) of Law No. 89/019 of 29 December 1989 modifying the 1972 Ordinance on Judicial Organization.

by some magistrates. In an effort to conform to the francophone region's use of the *juge des référés*, the anglophone courts have appointed the presidents of the courts of first instance of the place where execution takes place or where the judgement debtor resides or has domicile. Thus, the judge responsible for urgent matters will no longer be the president of the high court or of the court of appeal even if the litigation has progressed to this level. Because the presidents of the courts of first instance are nevertheless not granted a separate title analogous to the '*juge des référés*' that carries with it consequent separate authority, a president of a court of first instance now can, pursuant to Article 49, effectively reverse the decision of a high court, of a court of appeal, or even of the supreme court. There is evidence that presidents of courts of first instance have delved so far into the substance of the superior court's decision as to even modify the manner of payment. To emphasize – in this way, a relatively more junior and therefore likely less experienced lower court has effectively overturned the decision of a higher court. Of course, in the francophone region the *juge des référés*, too, can in effect change the decision of a high court, but this judge has been specifically appointed to the role, with an opportunity for the appointing authorities to take into account a candidate's knowledge and experience.

Because proper execution of judgements is of great importance to predictability and hence to commerce, every effort needs to be made to have maximum judicial experience brought to bear on questions of execution, and, generally, to enhance OHADA's uniformity. This is critical if OHADA is to succeed in facilitating commerce. At some point, appropriate legal facts may bring this issue before the CCJA, which will need to find a solution. Instead of waiting for this eventuality, the OHADA member states should modify their own institutions so that they do not impede OHADA's purpose of facilitating commerce. Consequently, the common law courts in anglophone Cameroon should consider appointing a specific, well-experienced judge to the role of '*juge des référés*', and all OHADA jurisdictions should similarly review their procedures.

Bailiffs and sheriffs, too, are critical to execution of judgements. These officials are at the centre of execution of court decisions and are sometimes allowed to seize the courts directly in cases of difficulties of execution. As is the case with magistrates and judges, impropriety exhibited by some bailiffs will reduce predictability and thus be a brake on commerce and investment. The enforcement agents, that is, bailiffs and sheriffs, again like magistrates and judges, are employees of the state. Because their actions are under the jurisdiction of the Procureur Général, that is, the Chief State Attorney, the OHADA Treaty requires the state to cause this official to supervise the enforcement agents in a manner compatible with OHADA laws.

Contracts for the Carriage of Goods by Road

This Uniform Act is the most recent and entered into force on 1 January 2004. The Uniform Act is based on the Convention on the Contract for the International Carriage of Goods by Road (CMR), Geneva, 19 May 1956. It concerns transport by road, which is critical to many developing countries; the Uniform Act was promulgated by the Council of Ministers to provide important coverage, since OHADA member states are not party to that convention.

The new OHADA law is applicable to contracts where a carrier undertakes as the principal obligation, for remuneration, to carry by vehicle and by road goods that are entrusted to the carrier by another person. Goods are defined as any movable goods that can be traded.

The Uniform Act requires the shipper (the natural or juridical person who sends the goods) to provide certain documents for customs, packaging, declarations and instructions, relating to the performance of the contract, inspection of the goods, delivery, payment and liability. There are provisions dealing with situations where several carriers transport the goods consecutively, using either the same type or different types of transport. The law also has provisions on rights of action, jurisdiction and arbitration.

The Problem of Interpretation of Laws

The adoption of any law, be it uniform or not, does not come with any guaranty as to its effectiveness. Legal rules are framed and formulated by legislators. They are frequently expressed in general terms and they call for a process of interpretation. In this regard, the role of the judge in the common law and civil law systems is relevant and significant. The questions: Can OHADA provide a bridge between common law and civil law systems? Is OHADA compatible with common law? Does OHADA possess the capacity to deal with the diversity of legal and judicial traditions of Africa?

The answers to these questions will be affirmative only if the courts of the OHADA member states apply the OHADA laws with an eye to OHADA's goal – to facilitate commerce. Specifically, the courts therefore must work to enhance OHADA's reduction of transaction costs by respecting its laws' uniformity, their support of transparency and their consistency with best commercial practices. The CCJA's decision in the *SEHIC* case is an example of a decision that strives to satisfy those requirements. This is how OHADA will continue to evolve as a living law appropriate to its economic and commercial environment.

The OHADA regime, for all its civil law inspiration, appreciates the importance of judicial interpretation of the Uniform Acts. That, after all, is the purpose of the CCJA. This institution's role is to protect the uniformity of the Acts in the context of the goals expressed by the OHADA Treaty. National-court magistrates and judges who render decisions on OHADA, as the judicial branch of member states, have the same responsibility as judges of the CCJA. The best method to ensure this reality is to take a page from the common law courts and to have every single decision concerning OHADA publicly available promptly after it has been handed down. This would permit each court to look at what other courts have done, and it would allow academics to comment on decisions, thereby contributing directly their knowledge and perspective as well. For this purpose, all decisions, both from the national courts and of course from the CCJA, must be systematically collected for publication and distribution, both in volumes, and over the Internet in fully searchable form.

Conclusion

OHADA is the law in Cameroon. Certainly to a common law jurist, it is already more than a handful of institutions and mere texts, because it is being deployed by practitioners and interpreted by the judiciary. As this chapter reflects, OHADA shows some flexibility and increasing maturity, but always based on the structure described in Chapter 3. The next chapter focuses on some issues particularly salient to a lawyer trained in the common law.

5

OHADA as Experienced in Cameroon: Addressing Areas of Particular Concern to Common Law Jurists

Martha Simo Tumnde, née Njikam, PhD
Associate Professor of Law and Dean, Faculty of Social and Management Sciences, University of Buea, Barrister and Solicitor of the Supreme Court of Cameroon[1]

The private sector demands an adequate legal framework that is sufficiently clear, modern, predictable and transparent to permit investments with a sense of security. It is against this background that OHADA[2] (Organization for the Harmonization in Africa of Business Law) was created by the treaty of Port Louis in Mauritius on 17 October 1993. The OHADA initiative is an emerging tool, which could progressively become

[1] This paper was presented at an international conference in Paris, *Place de Droit*, on the theme *'La Convergence du droit et globalisation des affaires'* organized by the Paris Bar Association from 15–17 November 2005.

[2] OHADA is the French acronym for l'Organisation pour l'Harmonisation en Afrique du Droit des Affaires. The treaty was initially signed by 14 countries: Benin, Burkina Faso, Cameroon, Central African Republic, Chad, Comoros, Congo, Côte d'Ivoire, Equatorial Guinea, Gabon, Mali, Niger, Senegal and Togo. Subsequently, Guinea (Conakry) and Guinea-Bissau joined, bringing the total to 16. It will soon be 17 should the Democratic Republic of Congo finally join. By virtue of Article 53, the treaty is open to all members of the African Union.

the common business law in anglophone and francophone African countries, taking the best from the civil law and common law systems.[1]

Pre-OHADA, Cameroon had made no effort to modernize its business laws and continued to rely on colonial laws. Outside the business-law arena, anglophone Cameroon continues to apply common law, doctrines of equity and pre-1900 statutes of general application by virtue of Section 11 of the Southern Cameroons High Court Law 1955 and pre-1960 Nigerian laws. In francophone Cameroon, French and French-derived laws promulgated in French Equatorial Africa before 1 January 1924 are applicable by virtue of decrees of 16 April and 24 May 1924. As a result of these temporal limitations, legal developments in England and France have not been extended to Cameroon. After many years of independence, Cameroon and certain other African countries continue to apply legislation which has long been abandoned in the countries where they were originally enacted. African states, with a few exceptions, are noted for their reluctance or total indifference to law reform. It is not uncommon to find evocations in our courts of outdated statutes such as the Sale of Goods Act 1893, Partnership Act 1890, Factors Act 1882, Company Ordinance 1958, Civil Code 1804 and the Commercial Code 1807.

Section 11 of the Southern Cameroons High Court Law 1955 and similar enactments in French-speaking Cameroon were essentially transitory, with the expectation that more appropriate and suitable local laws would be introduced subsequently. Law must keep pace with changing circumstances; they should evolve with society. OHADA may be the medium of redemption[2] for the member countries that might not otherwise have contemplated reform in the nearest future.

Today, in the third millennium, we are in a global village. Through electronic communication, it is possible to engage in international trade with persons from any part of the world from one's bedroom. The desire to catch the train of globalization has accelerated the process of reform in recent years.[3] One of the aspects of globalization is the desire to eliminate

---

[1] The OHADA Treaty and its Uniform Acts are truly a legal revolution in Africa, given the number of countries concerned, its scope and the matters at issue. It is an ambitious project. It consists of a corpus of texts called Uniform Acts, covering the following eight areas of business law: General Commercial Law, Commercial Companies and Economic Interest Groups, Accounting Law, Collective Proceedings for the Clearing of Debts, Securities Law, Simplified Recovery Procedures and Measures of Enforcement, Arbitration, and Contracts for the Carriage of Goods by Road.

[2] Dickerson, C.M. (2005) Harmonising business laws in Africa: OHADA Calls the Tune, *Columbia Journal of Transnational Law*, 44:17–73. See also, Tumnde-Njikam, M.S., 'The Future of OHADA in the age of Globalisation, paper presented at the OHADA Conference in Accra, Ghana, on 4 November 2003.

[3] Forneris, X. (2001) Harmonising Commercial Law in Africa: The OHADA, *Revue de Droit et de Science Politique* 47, p 77.

as much as possible the differences between the commercial laws in a particular region.

This is done in order to ensure as much as possible that the same rules apply to companies investing in that region. It would be more comforting if a Nigerian who wants to open a business in Cameroon, Côte d'Ivoire, Ghana, or any part of the African continent encountered identical rules of the game. The OHADA project clearly goes in this direction and represents an African answer to the challenge of globalization in the area of business law.

This chapter examines the applicability of the OHADA Treaty in Cameroon and thereby provides an insight into some of the practical problems of implementation, most particularly for jurisdictions of common law tradition.

Problems of Implementation

The OHADA has been in existence now since 1993 and has begun to make imprints in Cameroon, including anglophone Cameroon. The OHADA Treaty has been considered revolutionary and controversial in anglophone Cameroon for various reasons.[1] First, most of the consternation expressed related to the manner in which the treaty was thrust upon the business and legal environment in Cameroon, without any consideration for our national peculiarities and without much consultation or discussion with stakeholders and potential users of this law. There was insufficient national participation in the law-making process as the decision was made unilaterally by the head of state.

The applicability of the OHADA Treaty and Uniform Acts, too, raised constitutional issues in Cameroon. Specifically, OHADA's language aroused debates on the constitutionality of the provisions of the OHADA Treaty within the context of bilingual and bijural Cameroon.[2]

---

[1] There were elaborate discussions on the constitutionality of the OHADA Treaty in Cameroon at the OHADA Seminar on the theme: 'The Applicability of the OHADA Treaty in Cameroon', see, Proceedings of the OHADA Seminar held at the University of Buea, Buea, Cameroon, 18–19 September 2003. For the first time in Cameroon, this seminar brought together jurists from both common law and civil law provinces of Cameroon. This cross-border gathering was the springboard for multi-lingualism. It is worth noting that there is a proposed amendment to Article 42 of the OHADA Treaty currently under discussion. If adopted, it will usher in a multi-lingual dimension to the OHADA project: four languages, French, English, Spanish and Portuguese, shall be the working languages of OHADA; see Appendix 3.

[2] Article 1 (3) of Law No. 96-06 of 18 January 1996 to amend the Constitution of 2 June 1972; Tumnde-Njikam, M.S. (2002) The applicability of the OHADA Treaty in Cameroon: problems and prospects, *Annals of the Faculty of Law and Political Sciences*, 6, pp 23–32; See also, Tabe, S.T. (2002) Some antipodal hurdles that beset the uniform working of the OHADA Uniform Acts in Cameroon, *Annals of the Faculty of Law and Political Science*, 6, pp 33–43.

Article 42 of the treaty states that the working language of the treaty is French. The treaty and the Uniform Acts are drafted and issued in French. Implicitly, any document in English or any other language would be a translation from French to English or Spanish or Portuguese. Most of the texts in translation have been criticized for being literal, inadequate and rather nebulous. They are simply approximations, and in many cases there are no legal equivalents in English. There is a need for co-drafting of future OHADA Uniform Acts in order to avoid translation. Furthermore, it would be desirable to have a co-revision team to work together on the existing Uniform Acts. This team should employ contextual meanings of terminologies and the adaptation approach to translation. Member states should develop an OHADA lexicon of words, phrases and concepts. This would go a long way in clarifying the misunderstandings of legal jargons and terminologies.

The new Article 42 proposed by treaty-revisions signed in Quebec on October 17, 2008, and, as this book goes to press, circulating to complete ratification, goes a long way to rectifying these issues. If adopted, it will add English, Spanish and Portuguese to French as working languages.[1] In the event of difference among the versions, however, the French version will control. Because translation, especially legal translation, affects concepts as well as mere words and phrases, the adequacy of the new Article 42 will depend on the quality of the actual translations. The creation of such teams of translators becomes yet more imperative as soon as the new Article 42 is effective.

Article 9 of the treaty states that the Uniform Acts should be published in the official gazette of contracting states. The Cameroonian Constitution requires that publications in the official gazette be in both French and English in order to reflect the bilingual character of the country. In the case of *Akiangan Fombin Sebastian v. Foto Joseph and others*,[2] Justice Ayah Paul makes the point that a treaty which is basically French suffers from self-exclusion from the English-speaking provinces. Following his reasoning, by implication the OHADA Treaty and its Uniform Acts cannot be applied in the English-speaking provinces of Cameroon. A question which is often asked is, what would happen to a case that leaves the courts in the English-speaking provinces of Cameroon to the CCJA (Common Court of Justice and Arbitration) in Abidjan since the proceedings and decisions of all courts below the CCJA would have been in English? Perhaps, the CCJA would refuse to entertain the matter until the treaty's Article 42 no longer constitutes French the only working language of

---

[1] An English translation of these revisions is at Appendix 3.
[2] Suit No. HCK/3/96 of 6 January 2000 (Unreported).

OHADA; perhaps, in the interim, the CCJA could distinguish between a working language and an official language, and find some compromise to allow documents to be submitted in their original language. In the same vein, it may be assumed that, strictly applied, OHADA does not allow the courts in the English-speaking provinces of Cameroon to articulate in English, at least until the amendment to Article 42 does add English (along with Portuguese and Spanish) as a working language.

In the English-speaking provinces of Cameroon, the treaty was originally seen as an instrument of French, and francophone-Cameroonian neo-colonialism, since it ignored the bilingual and bijural nature of the country. Today, however, the reality is that, even before adoption of the amendment adding languages, official OHADA documents, including the treaty and the Uniform Acts, are translated from the French, although the French version remains the authentic and correct document. For the moment, pragmatism in addition to Article 42 demands this reference back to the original French, because of problems relating to translation of words, phrases and concepts from one language to another. The habit of referring back to the French will have to continue, of course, even if the currently circulating treaty revisions are fully ratified: as noted above, the French version would remain the controlling text in the event of differences.

If that is the focus concerning Cameroonian bilingualism, issues of OHADA in Cameroon are further compounded by the fact that the country is bijural, with common law and civil law operating parallel to each other in the anglophone and francophone provinces, respectively. The Uniform Acts are strongly grounded in civil law: except for the anglophone provinces of Cameroon, the OHADA member states share a tradition of civil law. Consequently, the common law jurists are braced for a novel legal battle. It is not surprising that there have been evocations such as 'What common law is left?' and 'Is OHADA common law friendly?'[1]

OHADA has even been described as an 'unruly horse'.[2] At an International Conference in Lagos in 2004,[3] participants asked questions such as what were the drafters of the OHADA Treaty harmonizing since they were dealing with basically civil law. In fact, even in OHADA's francophone region the countries had different business laws, albeit based on the same civil law heritage: some had updated pre-independence legal

[1] See keynote address by Akere Muna, Is OHADA 'Common Law Friendly?', in Proceedings of the OHADA Seminar held at the University of Buea, Buea, Cameroon, 18–19 September 2003, pp 7–16.

[2] Nko-Njoya, I. (2003) OHADA Treaty – An Unruly Horse, The Impartial Judge, No. 1, at p 21.

[3] See Report on the First OHADA International Conference, held on 30 April 2004 at Lagos Airport Hotel, Ikeja, Lagos, Nigeria.

regimes more than others; consequently, even among francophone countries, harmonization through OHADA has been meaningful.[1]

Nevertheless, the conference participants' interrogation of OHADA's usefulness is representative of early reactions of anglophone lawyers in Cameroon, as there is a certain degree of nostalgia for common law amongst the English-speaking jurists.[2] Some in Cameroon have argued that the bijural nature of the country ought to be preserved and promoted; that any meaningful reform should take into consideration Cameroon's national peculiarities. There is no reason to believe that another jurisdiction having an Anglo-Saxon legal tradition would be instinctively any more willing to replace its system with a civilian legal system.

Another main concern relating to the OHADA Treaty is that member states are required to renounce their legislative and judicial sovereignty in matters relating to business law.[3] The OHADA reform does in fact entail a transfer of sovereignty: for example, a supranational body, the Council of Ministers, not the national parliaments, adopts the Uniform Acts; the CCJA in Abidjan, and not the national supreme courts, is the final court of justice. This has generated criticism and unease among those who contend that parliamentarians and the supreme courts of member states have become moribund. The resistance is buttressed by the fact that parliamentarians are elected officials, whereas the Ministers of Justice and Finance who make up the Council of Ministers are appointees of the member states.

One response to this criticism is that OHADA refers only to business laws and that, consequently, the contracting parties do not in fact give up much sovereignty. Another is that, if the OHADA Treaty had been

---

1 For a description of the state of pre-OHADA business laws even in francophone West and Central Africa, consider also Julie Paquin (2001) *L'harmonisation du droit des affaires en Afrique; le projet de l'OHADA*, Ohadata D-04-15 [Online] www.ohada.com; http://www.barreau.qc.ca/publications/journal/vol33/no15/ohada.html (last visited 18 April 2008)

2 The university of Buea played host to three international seminars: The Applicability of the OHADA Treaty in Cameroon, 18–19 September 2003; The Implementation of the OHADA Accounting System: Practice, Problems and Prospects, 15–16 September 2005; The Implementation of the Uniform Act on Simplified Recovery Procedures and Measures of Execution in Cameroon: Practice, Problems and Prospects, 15–16 November 2005. It has organized five workshops on various themes: The Implementation of the OHADA Treaty and Uniform Acts in Cameroon, April 2003, by a student body called the Law Society; Implementation of the Uniform Act on General Commercial Law: Practice, Problems and Prospects, hosted by FAKLA (Fako Lawyers Association), Limbe, 30 October 2005; Implementation of the Uniform Acts on General Commercial Law, Bankruptcy, Securities and Simplified Recovery Procedures and Measures of Execution, hosted by the BALA (Bamenda Lawyers Association), Bamenda, 30 December 2005; Implementation of the Uniform Act on Company Law, hosted by University of Douala, Faculty of Law, 10 December 2005 and Implementation of the Uniform Acts: Problems and the Way forward, hosted by MELA (Meme Lawyers Association), 16 January 2006. These seminars and workshops have served as a very useful resource channel for the information put together in this paper.

3 See Articles 6, 10, 14 and 20 of the treaty on the Harmonization in Africa of Business Law (See Appendix 2).

properly adopted in Cameroon, it would obviate the question about the Council of Ministers' legitimacy for acts applicable to Cameroon: the will of the people, as expressed in the Constitution, has been respected. Thus, it will be important for any future adhering states to respect all procedural requirements.

At a different level, the OHADA national commissions have evolved *sua sponte* as an interface both between the government and the Council of Ministers and between the national governments and the jurists and businesspeople most directly affected by the OHADA laws. Contracting states have begun to recognize that these commissions are very important to OHADA's functioning and legitimacy: acting through the Council of Ministers, they have sought to formalize the commissions, as further discussed in Chapter 7.

Despite their importance, commission members are appointed by the executive, not elected by the people. Of course, freely elected parliamentarians can be unimpressive and lack independence, and judges and ministers appointed by the executive can be both skilful and independent. However, it is inevitable that the calibre of all these professionals, as well as the members of the national commissions, may be compromised and that the current selection processes may result in allegiance and mediocrity.

With respect to judges in particular, anglophone Cameroonian legal professionals are particularly concerned as they argue that the common law's tradition of elevating accomplished barristers to the bench explains why the supreme courts of most common law countries harbour the most skilled and experienced judges, who, in consequence, are able to withstand external pressures. These anglophone sceptics view with dismay the OHADA requirement that decisions of the High Courts and Courts of Appeal be appealed directly to the CCJA, thereby bypassing the most learned and esteemed jurists. For some anglophones, the cost of losing access to the most respected jurists exceeds the benefits to be extracted from uniformity in interpretation of the business laws.

For all the criticism, the CCJA is a very important and innovative institution, which lies at the heart of the OHADA system. The CCJA has its headquarters at Abidjan, Côte d'Ivoire. While many non-Ivoirian lawyers fear that litigating before the CCJA is very expensive because litigants and lawyers based in other member states must travel to Abidjan to plead their cause before the CCJA, members of the CCJA have informally reminded the legal profession in the OHADA territory that the OHADA Treaty and CCJA procedures do not require either a trip to Abidjan or representation by an Ivoirian lawyer. Because the CCJA uses a civil law–inspired procedure, its decisions are based on dossiers. These can be sent by post to the CCJA's chief clerk. Thus, if lawyers from contracting states other than Côte d'Ivoire were willing to forgo the seemingly superfluous personal presence of the litigants or their representatives, the benefit of reduction of transaction costs brought by OHADA would no longer be offset by the expense of appeal to the CCJA. Because of this misunderstanding, in Cameroon, for example, many cases do not go beyond the Courts of Appeal in various provinces because of the fear of costs involved.

When jurists consider alternatives to the CCJA's current procedures, they note that by its Article 19 of the Rules of Procedure, the CCJA may, if it deems it necessary, meet in any member state with the latter's prior consent and without any financial burden for the state. This is discretionary and not mandatory. Unless legal professionals become uniformly comfortable with the CCJA's appeal process, this court may find it desirable to amend its rules, for example to make the CCJA touring courts and/or be permanently established in each member state attached to a special bench, for example, the Commercial Bench of the Supreme Court. Again, assuming that litigants and legal professionals continue to fear the current procedure, this would bring the court nearer to the people and allay the fears of poor litigants who do not have the means to travel to Abidjan. In this way, it would provide greater access to justice.

These and other alternatives are under consideration, but of course each of these options carries its own costs. Because the CCJA can speak only when it receives a question in proper form from a permitted interlocutor, a contracting state would be advised to formally interrogate the court regarding its procedure. In that way, lawyers within the OHADA territory, especially those trained in the common law system and thus not used to a purely written procedure, would be able to reassure themselves and their own clients as to the reliability and advantages of the CCJA's non-oral appeals.

The CCJA raises other concerns for common law jurists. Since the CCJA is currently made up exclusively of judges trained under the civil law, there is need to appoint common law trained judges. Anglophones of Cameroonian extraction are best suited to serve on the CCJA for the purpose of handling issues which may arise involving common law from anglophone Cameroon.

Another concern is a paucity of trained personnel. A lot of the misapprehensions and misunderstandings within anglophone Cameroon concerning the OHADA laws stem from the fact that very few jurists are sufficiently skilled in business law and comparative law to advise clients and judge cases efficiently under OHADA. For example, a lawyer trained under the common law cannot overnight be cast into the civil law mould and be competent to plead before the CCJA, whether orally or in writing. The Regional Training Centre for Legal Officers (ERSUMA) is located at Porto Novo in Benin. It is a laudable idea that there be a training school, but it falls short of the needs of anglophone lawyers trained in the common law tradition. The school is centralized, and training is limited to a few; it seeks to diffuse widely knowledge about OHADA and its laws by 'training the trainers'. A legal professional who obtains an ERSUMA certificate is expected to share the acquired knowledge upon returning home. For anglophones, however, the first hurdle is that, currently, the training in Benin is in French; other languages could profitably have been added before, but will need to be included upon the revision of Article 42 to include English, as well as Spanish and Portuguese, as working languages. There is very specifically a need to train lawyers of Anglo-Saxon legal heritage using the English language as the medium of expression. This may require a substantial change in ERSUMA's programme and orientation in order to meet the needs and aspirations of a common law lawyer.

Much more generally, and not applicable only to anglophones dealing with French-influenced substantive laws and procedures, OHADA still lacks the basic infrastructure necessary to make it an efficient tool for the achievement of transparency and predictability. OHADA needs structural adjustment. Arguably, the creation of the Trade and Personal Property Credit Registry (commercial registry) is one of the greatest innovations brought forth by the OHADA initiative: the OHADA laws reflect the intention that the commercial registry centralize publication of security interests, business assets and information relative to business organizations, as well as identification of commercial operators. However, in recent times, the commercial registries of Yaounde, Douala, Limbe, Buea, Kumba, Tiko and Bamenda have come under a barrage of criticisms. The consequent difficulties of enforcement are lamentable, and practical problems faced by commercial operators are many.

The commercial registry has not fully achieved its objectives of ensuring legal security because of inefficiency, maladministration and lack of basic infrastructure. For example, there is lack of unanimity in the registration procedure, and the contents of information required in the forms vary from one jurisdiction to another. There is as yet no well-organized and equipped commercial registry in Cameroon. There are no files of registered companies, only a ledger of entries of registered companies. There are no computers and skilled employees. Commercial operators are plagued by delay and inefficiency. The registration process is slow. This delay is often caused by inadequate personnel, inadequate facilities and crude registration process. It is scandalous that in the 21st century, an age of information and communications technology, registration of companies is done manually. Time is of the essence in business transactions. If the system operates in a slow and inefficient manner, it retards instead of promoting investments. This problem is further compounded by the fact that most of the employees at the commercial registry are not versed in basic legal terminologies, such as pledges, bonds, shares, stocks. The grim picture experienced at the commercial registry is one of corruption and of administrative and bureaucratic bottlenecks. The employees intentionally delay the registration process if extra money is not paid to them.

One of the functions of the commercial registry is to ensure that commercial operators comply with the provisions of Article 42 of the Uniform Act on General Commercial Law. This article stipulates that where a corporate body or natural person fails to apply for registration within the time limit, the competent court may itself, or at the request of the registrar in charge of the commercial registry or of any other person, take a decision compelling the party concerned to register. However, the courts have not acted in this vein and registrars rarely verify whether companies or commercial operators have complied with the necessary registration process.

A good example is the case of the CDC (Cameroon Development Corporation) in Limbe, which roughly 10 years after OHADA's company law came into effect, still had not registered with the Court of First Instance in Limbe. This of course may lead to uncertainty and irregularity within the system. It is commonplace to find companies and natural persons operating without authorization or any modification in status. There is an indifference to the requirement for registration. Most commercial operators are unaware of its implications for themselves, others and the nation. Registration is viewed as a formality and not an obligation. Evidently, this would have a rippling effect on the system, such as perpetration of illegal contracts and reduction of investors' confidence. It is clear that the objectives of OHADA are under threat because of the practical realities on the ground. This lack of basic infrastructure defeats the objectives of transparency and predictability.

The Way Forward

With regard to the uniformization of laws under OHADA, important questions must be asked: Does OHADA take into consideration African cultural and traditional norms? It would seem that if it does not, then the integration process will be an uneasy marriage. Can the bijural nature of Cameroon be preserved, let alone promoted, within the context of OHADA? Can meaningful reform take into consideration the national peculiarities? Importantly, can OHADA accommodate the contradictory conditions of contemporary society, and the challenges of globalization and modernization? The appropriate approach should be to promote such laws, principles and practices that accord with the orthodox and universally accepted standards of justice and fairness modified to suit Cameroonians and in fact African realities.

Although the law should naturally reflect the ideas and orientation of the law makers, it will not succeed if it only imposes, or appears to impose, some abstract justice that takes no account of the culture, traditions and aspirations of those on whom it will be administered. Experience has shown that hasty moves to destroy one community in favour of the other, or to dragoon one into the other in the bid for unity have always been short-lived. The reform process ought to envisage that the two legal systems in the anglophone and francophone provinces of Cameroon will continue to exist like permanent birthmarks. It is hoped that this new legislation will help build stronger bridges between legal traditions and cultures on the African continent. It should overcome the traditional distinction between common law and civil law systems, while respecting the role to be played by the traditional law within the context of African legal systems.

It is worth noting that OHADA authorizes arbitration as a method to resolve disputes and thereby provides a method to remove commercial cases from the court system. Negotiation, conciliation and arbitration are typical strategies for conflict management and resolution in African culture. This emphasis on conciliation and arbitration reflects and seeks to give life to the aspirations of the people as a whole and to take into consideration the needs of the African countries and their economies, as distinct from the needs of the more developed countries.

It seems imperative to create an enabling environment so that the Cameroonian legal system can align to the legal notions and instruments of OHADA, to the extent that these are better adapted to current commercial realities. The purpose of OHADA is to create a single legal environment that would avoid problems of conflict of laws and therefore foster investment. Although this articulated purpose focuses on foreign investment, the implementation of its goals of clarity, transparency and predictability can support domestic investment as well. For lawyers, convergence of business laws opens up corporate practice within the entire region. Within the OHADA territory, law professors can teach business law in any university; so long as OHADA law governs a conflict, members of the judiciary can with ease sit on the commercial bench of courts in any contracting state.

Understanding the intricacies and complexities of any new legal dispensation is not an easy task, especially at its advent. The question one may ask is, 'Is it OHADA which is the issue or its implementation which is a problem?' The commercial registry, for example, is an important innovation whose effectiveness is threatened not because of a failure inherent to OHADA, but because the national systems have not allocated the resources necessary to permit it to work as designed. The problem may in fact not be the laws themselves but their implementation. Perhaps especially in a bilingual and bijural country such as Cameroon, there is an urgent need to organize seminars, workshops and refresher courses for potential stakeholders and beneficiaries of this law. Continuing legal education and short courses are recommended for employees at the commercial registry in order to keep them abreast of the current legal developments. Adequate facilities must be put in place for the common law lawyer to operate within the OHADA context.

On a very practical level, there is need for a bilingual OHADA code commentary, OHADA lexicon and publications on OHADA to foster the dissemination of knowledge and information on a current body of law. The OHADA laws and comparative law ought to be widely taught in schools and universities. Outreach and networking within professional associations and cross-border activities must be encouraged and fostered.

For example, the Fako Lawyers Association in the Southwest Province's city of Limbe has created an OHADA club and is networking within the neighbouring African countries for the dissemination of information on the OHADA Treaty, Uniform Acts and decisions of the CCJA and Council of Ministers. It may be necessary that the Permanent Secretariat establish branch offices, libraries and resource centres in member states for the dissemination of publications on OHADA. In addition, for the commercial registry to perform its function expediently and efficiently, its structure must be revamped. A sophisticated computerized system is imperative. The OHADA Permanent Secretariat and a small working group, including a judge from the CCJA, were assigned the task of determining the criteria for the necessary software. The proposed software is known as *logiciels GAGI*,[1] which is just beginning to be implemented in limited areas of the OHADA territory. The current infrastructural limitation, including the

[1] The term 'logiciel' is the French for 'software'; 'GAGI' is an economic interest group, and the name stands for 'Groupement d'Automatisation des Greffes par l'Informatique'.

shortage of skilled personnel, makes the task of the commercial registry impossibly onerous and puts it in an insidious position.

In the interim, a special commercial registry should be created in each Court of First Instance, with instructions to cross-index information and to centralize information as much as physically possible. Further, a department should be created at the level of the Ministry of Justice to carry out periodic spot checks concerning the filing and presentation of documents.[1]

At minimum, the careful structure and drafting of OHADA puts into high relief the deficiencies of the national judicial systems; at maximum, OHADA provides a sophisticated and clear package of business laws, uniform across a large territory. Through the efforts of the University of Buea, of practicing attorneys and of the judiciary, the anglophone region of Cameroon is in the process of implementing OHADA. We are already seeing how it is promoting and facilitating commerce in the region, and that, with additional and continuing national support, OHADA will be able to live up to its promise even in a region whose legal tradition is the common law.

Conclusion

As the Cameroonian experience demonstrates, harmonization of business laws in Africa through OHADA is a significant step towards overcoming traditional distinctions, at least between the common law and the civil law systems. These elegantly drafted statutory provisions must be enforced, however, to be effective. The task is not Herculean since, in the field of business law, both of these northern-inspired legal systems seek to provide and reinforce predictability: business law is one area where the traditional line separating civil law and common law is blurred. Even the Uniform Acts relating to General Commercial Law, Securities and Guaranties, and Commercial Companies, which are the OHADA laws that have taken the most from civil law, adumbrate principles very similar to those under the common law. Other OHADA Uniform Acts themselves are products of convergence of laws. For example, in the area of accounting, transportation of goods by road, and arbitration, the Uniform Acts display a move towards international standards.

[1] This inspiration can be drawn from the provisions of the CIMA Code. The Ministry of Finance, Department of Insurance, carries out periodic controls of insurance companies. These controls include inspection at the place of business of insurance companies and inspection of documents. See further, Tumnde-Njikam, M.S. (2003) *Motor Vehicle Insurance Law in Cameroon*, Design House, Limbe, Cameroon, pp 232–261.

Inevitably, OHADA affects each contracting state's sovereignty but only with respect to business laws. If that is the cost, in Africa as in Europe the increasing number of multilateral agreements concerning business reflect a growing consensus in favour of some relinquishment of sovereignty in exchange for uniformization. The experience of the EU (European Union), ECOWAS (Economic Community of West African States), CEMAC (*Communauté Economique et Monétaire d'Afrique Centrale*) and other regional bodies confirms that unless the states give up part of their national sovereignty and empower regional institutions to make binding decisions, and to implement them, little progress can be achieved. Harmonization of business law in Africa falls naturally within the framework of the objectives of these and other regional and continent-wide organizations. It is clearly in the interest of Africa eventually to have a single and uniform law all over the region. Among anglophones, among lawyers trained in the common law, Cameroon is the testing ground, the laboratory for this experience.

6

Simplified Recovery Procedures and Measures of Execution: A Nigerian Perspective on OHADA

The late Professor John Ademola Yakubu, PhD
Professor of Law, University of Ibadan, Ibadan, Nigeria
Edited posthumously by Claire Moore Dickerson

Unless the law is enforced, its elegance and sophistication are useless. For this reason, the mechanism for recovery in the event of non-performance deserves separate analysis. As a proxy for all such recoveries, let us compare recovery mechanisms under Nigerian law and OHADA law, in the event that the debtor resists paying the obligation.

Recovery of Debt Under Common Law

Under Nigerian common law, a debt can be recovered through the debtor's simple payment. This does not call for any elaborate comment as the debtor's acknowledgement of a debt owed to the creditor is implicit in the debtor's payment of that debt. A payment of it, except there are other ancillary issues, discharges the debtor of the debt.

Where however a debtor disputes the debt or accepts the debt but is tardy in the payment of it, the creditor who chooses to go to court for the purpose of pursuing the claim against the debtor, could ask for the issuance of a writ and filing of a statement of claim or proceed to an undefended list action or garnishee proceedings or request an injunction. Each of these is considered in turn.

Non-jurisdictional substantive and procedural concerns

Writ of summons and statement of claim

The most common method of pursuing a debt claim is through the writ of summons in court and a statement of claim. The defendant is expected to file a statement of defence if any defence to the action will be claimed. The writ of summons must be sought for in court and the statement of claim must be filed in the high court, although paltry claims can be pursued in the magistrates' court. Where a statement of defence is filed, the matter may proceed to trial at the end of which the court gives its judgement based on the consideration of the pleadings and evidence adduced in the pursuit of the claim and the defence. Where a party feels aggrieved by the decision of the court, the aggrieved party may appeal to the Court of Appeal and ultimately up to the highest court in the relevant common law jurisdiction.

Upon obtaining a judgement, it must be executed. The writ of attachment and sale of property (*fieri facias*, or FiFa) is the most popular of the enforcement measures under Nigerian common law. By this method, the property of the judgement debtor is attached and sold for the purpose of making good the debt. Nigeria being a federated state, enforcement of judgements even within the country is first limited by the jurisdiction of the relevant court; consider Cap 407 of the Laws of the Federation of Nigeria 1990, the statute that governs enforcement of judgements in Nigeria. The title of the Act states that the Act has been enacted to make provision for 'the appointment and duties of sheriffs, the enforcement of judgements and orders and the service and execution of civil process of the courts throughout Nigeria'.

The Act requires that each state appoint a Sheriff[1] and a Deputy Sheriff.[2] The sheriffs appoint such number of persons as bailiffs as may be necessary.[3] The sheriffs are expected to receive writs and processes of court.[4] The Act provides that any sum of money payable under a judgement of a court may be recovered, in case of default, or failure of payment thereof forthwith or at the same time or times and in the manner thereby

1 See Section 3 of Cap 407 LFN 1990.
2 See Section 4 of Cap 407 LFN 1990.
3 See Section 5 of Cap 407 LFN 1990.
4 See Section 8 of Cap 407 LFN 1990.

directed, by execution against the goods and chattels and the immovable property of the judgement debtor in accordance with the provisions of the Act.[1] The Act requires that the registrar on the application of the judgement creditor cause to be issued a writ of attachment and sale whereby the sheriff is empowered to levy or cause to be levied by distress and sale of goods and chattels, wherever they may be found within the division or district of the court, the money payable under the judgement and the costs of the execution.[2]

Undefended list

The undefended list concerns debts allegedly not contestable by the debtor. It ensures that these debts are timeously disposed of by the use of a writ of summons and an affidavit stating facts that in the opinion of the creditor, the debtor will have no defence to his or her claim and that judgement should be entered for the creditor in line with the writ of summons. The basis for taking this action is usually stated in the affidavit. If the debtor has no defence to the action, judgement is entered for the creditor in line with the writ of summons. If the debtor however wishes to contest the claim, the only manner is by filing a counter affidavit. Where the court feels that the debt is contested and cannot be disposed of by the method of the undefended list, the matter will be transferred to the general cause list. The process of a whole trial will then have to be embarked upon.

For example, Order 23 of the High Court Civil Procedure Rules of Oyo State of Nigeria relating to 'Undefended list' allocates to the court the authority to review first the plaintiff's application for a writ of summons and then, if the court allows the suit to be entered on the 'Undefended List', the court subsequently reviews any defendant's determination to defend.

In *Bank of the North v. Intra Bank S.A.*,[3] the Supreme Court of Nigeria stated the object of the undefended list to be 'quick dispatch of certain cases, eg, debt of liquidated money demand'. The supreme court also held thus: 'we reiterated that judgement entered in an undefended list is a judgement entered on the merits and is not a default judgement'.[4] The utility of the undefended list is quick dispensation of justice especially with respect to a debt or liquidated demand.

---

[1] See Section 20(1) of Cap 407 LFN 1990.
[2] See Section 20(2) of Cap 407 LFN 1990.
[3] (1969) All NLR 88.
[4] at p. 94

Garnishee proceedings

A garnishee proceeding is a method of execution by which a third-party debt owed a judgement debtor by another person is attached so that this third party is made to pay the debt of the judgement debtor to the judgement creditor. Thus, the parties to a garnishee proceeding are the judgement creditor who is known as the garnishor, the judgement debtor and, finally, the other person who owes the judgement debtor, known as the garnishee. It is usually an interlocutory proceeding.

In order to commence a garnishee proceeding, an affidavit must be filed by the garnishor. The affidavit must state the basis for asking the court to assume jurisdiction and to give the order. A copy of the judgement should be annexed to enable the court to appreciate the basis of the action of the garnishor. Leave of the court must be sought and obtained to commence a garnishee proceeding. Once the affidavit is filed, it constitutes an ex parte application for an order Nisi.[1]

Obi Okoye, writing on garnishee proceedings emphasized the effort made to balance the need for speed and the obligation of fairness to the garnishee and the judgement debtor.[2]

The effect of the service of the order Nisi on the garnishee is the attachment of the debt. The garnishee must therefore not pay the money to the judgement debtor. The amount the judgement creditor (garnishor) is entitled to should not be larger than the amount due by the judgement debtor, even if the total amount due to the judgement debtor by the garnishee is larger than the claim of the garnishor.

Obi Okoye, commenting further on the procedure to be adopted with respect to garnishee proceedings underscored that, to the extent the garnishee pays into the court the lesser of the amount owed to the judgement debtor or the latter's judgement debt, the garnishee is protected against later claims.[3] Put differently, a garnishee who does not question the garnishee's obligation to the judgement creditor can satisfy the obligation rapidly and at minimum cost, and is well protected by Nigerian law.

A garnishee who disputes an indebtedness to the judgement debtor must appear in court on the return date to state the basis for this objection. The objection must relate to cogent issues or facts. Defences that can be put up include the fact that the debt that is sought to be garnished belongs to a third party or to a person who has a charge or lien on it or a set off was due to the garnishee before the service of the order Nisi.

---

1 See Order VIII Sheriff and Civil Process Act Cap 407 Laws of the Federation of Nigeria.

2 See Okoye, O. (1986) *Essays on Civil Proceedings*, vol 11, Fourth Dimension Publishers, Nigeria, reprint.

3 See Okoye, O. (1986) *Essays on Civil Proceedings*, vol 11, Fourth Dimension Publishers, Nigeria, reprint.

Where there is no basis for the court not to make the order absolute, the court will do so. An absolute garnishee order is discretionary. Thus, it will not be granted where in the opinion of the court it is inequitable to do so. In *Barclays Bank D.C. O. v. Baderinwa*,[1] the court held that a garnishment order will not be made absolute where there is doubt as to whether the debt attached belongs to the judgement debtor absolutely; consequently, the garnishee's debt to the judgement debtor will not have been discharged, should the garnishor ultimately be authorized to proceed further there-with. The court in this case directed that an inquiry be made as to ownership of the debt.

Other methods of debt recovery

The Nigerian legal system offers other measures to recover a debt. Imagine, for example, that, given the state of business of the company, it is in the interest of the creditors that the company be wound up. Relief would constitute having the company wound up, and having the money due to the creditors of the company thus realized from the money derived from the sale of the assets of the company.

Jurisdictional Concerns Relating to Enforcement Measures

Within Nigeria

Nigeria being a federated state, a judgement creditor who needs to have the benefit of the judgement satisfied outside the jurisdiction of the court or outside the state may apply that the judgement be recognized by the other state. Section 104 of the Sheriffs and Civil Process Act provides that any person in whose favour a judgement has been given or made in a court of any state or the capital territory may obtain from the registrar or other proper officer of such court a certificate of such judgement.[2] Upon production of such certificate to the registrar or other proper officer of any court of like jurisdiction in any other state or the capital territory such officer must register the certificate in 'The Nigerian Register of Judge-ment'.[3] From the date of registration, the certificate is a record of the court

[1] (1962) All NLR 731.
[2] See Section 104 30(1) of Cap 407 LFN 1990.
[3] See Section 105(1) of Cap 407 LFN 1990.

in which it is registered and has the same force and effect as a judgement of that court.[1]

Outside Nigeria

A judgement creditor in pursuit of the enforcement of the judgement outside the country where the judgement was delivered may use the judgement as a basis of an action in another country. An obligation enforceable in one forum cannot normally be enforced in another without the institution of fresh legal proceedings.

A forum may also accept by statute or treaty reciprocal enforcement of some or all foreign judgements. Thus, in the case of Nigeria, by reason of the Foreign Judgements (Reciprocal Enforcement) Act 1960, foreign judgements of the countries that have ratified the reciprocal enforcement agreement are given recognition and enforcement so long as the judgement satisfies certain criteria.[2]

Simplified Recovery Procedures and Measures of Execution

Similarities between OHADA and Nigerian common law

Under the OHADA (Organization for Harmonization in Africa of Business Law) Uniform Act on simplified recovery procedures and measures of execution, the court can make one of two orders, that is, a traditional order to make payment, or the arguably more innovative order to deliver or to return an object.[3] In fact, analogous orders are obtainable under the common law. As we have just seen, the order to make payment, or even to deliver or to return an object, can be made by the court under the common law.

---

1 See Section 105(2) of Cap 407 LFN 1990. See also section 287(3) of the 1999 Constitution. It provides thus: 'The decisions of the Federal High Court, a High Court and of all other courts established by this constitution shall be enforced in any part of the Federation by all authorities and persons, and by other courts of law with subordinate jurisdiction to that of the Federal high court, a High Court and those other courts, respectively.'

2 The judgement must have been delivered by a superior court in the foreign country, it must have been registered within six years of delivery, it must be final and conclusive, it cannot be penal and any sum must have been liquidated.

3 See Boris Mator *et al* (2007) *Business Law in Africa, OHADA and the Harmonisation Process* (2nd edition), GMB Publishing Ltd., London & Philadelphia pp 234-35.

Other points of similarity include the fact that, under the OHADA Uniform Act, any measure must first be taken against the movable assets of the debtor. Section 25 of the Nigerian Sheriffs and Civil Process Act has a similar provision. OHADA makes provision for levying of execution on the immovables of the judgement debtor if the movables of the judgement debtor cannot satisfy the judgement debt. This is also the provision under Section 44 of the Sheriffs and Civil Process Act.

In summary, OHADA measures and Nigeria's common law measures are generally the same in scope, and they achieve the same result. The same can be said about the procedure for achieving the effect of each of these enforceable measures. For example, in Nigeria the high court rules and the Sheriffs and Civil Process Act are effective laws that achieve the same outcomes as do the OHADA provisions. Most of the interim or provisional measures under the common law are obtainable through the use of equitable principles, and the equitable principles' requirements that need be satisfied to obtain any of them justify their use in the same way as do OHADA measures in this respect.

OHADA's principles regarding the lifting of seizure are similar to those at common law, including as described in Section 22 of the Nigerian Sheriffs and Civil Process Act, provided that a judgement debtor can by payment satisfy the obligation and discharge the judgement before the judgement sale. As a general matter, both under OHADA and in the common law countries, all issues and principles relating to recovery of debt and enforcement measures limit the judgement creditor's recovery to the amount of the just claim.

Many of the provisions relating to assets with a third party and rights of a third party vis-à-vis the judgement creditor under OHADA are also recognized by the common law. Thus, measures such as garnishee proceedings and interpleaders summons are analogous to OHADA provisions.

With respect to preference of movable assets for seizure, the simplicity of execution against movables is favoured in both systems. For an immovable, the OHADA provisions respecting co-ownership of an immovable are also recognized in the common law system. The requirement of registration for the purpose of assuring better title, to warn intruders and to state the encumbrance on the immovable property under OHADA is also present under the common law.

Differences between OHADA and Nigerian Common Law

There are differences, of course, between OHADA and the common law, and they can seem quite strange. One such difference, for example, concerns the procedure for an auction sale. Under OHADA, such a sale is more elaborate, including a concededly archaic practice of timing the auction by the successive burning of three 1-minute candles. In fact, details do tend to differ – unsurprisingly, the time within which acts of the same nature ought to be done within the two systems are not necessarily the same. Even in all these areas of difference, however, OHADA remains clear and unambiguous.[1]

Other differences may seem more fundamental. Under the OHADA Uniform Act, the conditions for issuing an order to make payment are very explicit. The OHADA stipulation provides for domicile, actual residence of the debtor and contractual stipulation as alternative elements for assumption of jurisdiction. In most of the common law jurisdictions, service of the writ is enough for the court to assume jurisdiction, and it is the court that determines when the writ will issue. Lord Haldane in *John Russel & Co. v. Cayzen Irvine & Co Ltd.*[2] provides a sense for the common law judge's discretion when he notes that 'the root principle of English law about jurisdiction is that judges are in the place of the sovereign in whose name they administer justice and that therefore whoever is served with the king's writ ... is a person over whom the courts have jurisdiction.' The appropriate extent of judicial discretion is a complicated issue, of course.

Another difference is OHADA's emphasis on conciliation in the event the debtor disclaims the debt. At common law, conciliation is a different process altogether. It may, of course, be used before choosing to go to court but otherwise is available principally for divorce proceedings.[3]The question is whether OHADA's process will, even in a common law country, expedite the resolution of disputes. Alternate dispute resolution systems, a category to which conciliation belongs, are finding favor in developed countries of common law heritage, and they may be effective means of reducing the delays and costs seemingly inherent in classic litigation.

Another difference between OHADA and common law concerns the recognition and enforcement of judgements outside the issuing states that

[1] See Yakubu, A. (2003) *Law of Contract in Nigeria*, Malthouse Press, Lagos pp 9–10. See also Nickerson, H.V. (1873) L.R. Q.B. 286; and *Adebaje v. Conde* (1938) 19 NLR 57.

[2] (1966) 2 AC 298. See also *Colt v. Sarliet* (1966) 1 All ER 678.

[3] See the Arbitration and Conciliation Act of Nigeria, Cap 19 Laws of the Federation of Nigeria 1990.

delivered the judgements. In common law countries, except where there is a reciprocal enforcement statute, enforcement has to be by action. The uniform nature of the procedure is similar to the application of Nigerian procedure within its own borders, among its own federated states, but, of course, extends to other countries. That OHADA's uniformity crosses national borders is a significant difference and serves to reduce transaction costs.

Along the same lines, all of the basic OHADA rules relating to recovery of debts and enforcement measures for all OHADA member states are now to be found in the Uniform Act relating to simplified debt recovery procedures and measures of execution. To be sure, subsequent physical enforcement of the judgements is returned to the national governments under the simplified process, but the source of law is easier to identify than in common law countries. In Nigeria, for example, rules concerning execution of judgements are contained in the various High Court Civil Procedures Rules, Commercial Law Principles, Decided Cases, Sheriffs and Civil Process Act, Law of Contract Principles and Cognate Laws. The Nigerian Sheriffs and Civil Process Act is very elaborate with respect to differing methods of execution. Again, we have seen that the outcomes are similar between OHADA and common law, but for ease of access to applicable law, OHADA has the advantage.

Not only is the source within each common law country complicated, but the substantive law changes in unpredictable ways from one such country to the next. The same is true in respect of the various procedures in common law countries, even if the procedures are intended to achieve the same result in each jurisdiction. Underlying these complications is a general principle of common law that says issues of adjectival law are to be governed by the lex fori. In *Bank of the North vs. Intra Bank S.A.*[1], the Supreme Court of Nigeria, focusing specifically on the undefended list but appearing to assert a general proposition, underscored that there is no longer even a common point of departure with the former colonial power. There, the Court, per Ademola CJN stated that '... we have come to the conclusion that the rules governing the practice known as Undefended List must be considered in their own isolation and English practice and rules must not be brought in'.[2] In comparison, as is now obvious to the reader, the OHADA substantive and procedural law is identical across all its member states.

[1] (1969) ANLR 88.

[2] at p 93. In *R.V. Wallace Johnson* 5 WACA 56 it was held that a code should be construed in its application to the facts of the case free from any glosses or interpolations derived from any expositions, however authoritative.

To emphasize the uniformity offered by OHADA, remember that it applies not only to the texts of the Uniform Acts, but also to their interpretation. While the Common Court of Justice and Arbitration is the highest court for OHADA member states, the highest court of each common law country serves as the highest referral court for that country. Thus, while all the member states of OHADA truly do speak with one voice on simplified recovery of debt methods and measures of execution, in respect of the common law countries, it is a case of chacun pour soi, Dieu pour nous tous.

Conclusion

A comparison of simplified recovery of debt and enforcement measures under OHADA to their analogues under the common law reveals that there are many areas of convergence. There are differences as well.

The OHADA states enjoy uniformity of rules and procedures since the member states can boast of a single statute for recovery procedures and measures of enforcement. Each of the common law states has to contend with its own rules. Even where the concepts and rules are similar, they can differ in content and procedure for enforcement, and any lawyer knows that in the proper circumstances a tiny distinction can lead to an entirely different result.

Not only does OHADA offer the advantage of uniformity, but it also provides easy accessibility to the source of law, again because the relevant law is contained in an immediately identifiable Uniform Act.

The best part may be that a common law country can acquire the benefit of OHADA's uniformity and its ease of access without engaging in fundamental changes: the outcomes of OHADA law are substantially those available under the common law system. As the Cameroonian experience suggests, contemplating adoption of the OHADA simplified recovery procedures and measures of execution may be harder for common law trained jurists than is actually applying a Uniform Act whose consequences are substantially similar to outcomes under common law.

7

Perspectives on the Future

Claire Moore Dickerson
Sen. John B. Breaux Professor of Law, Tulane University Law School

The future of OHADA (Organization for Harmonization in Africa of Business Law) is necessarily determined by its past. So long as OHADA is successful, it defines its own future. It thus is important to identify OHADA's goals and to compare them against OHADA's accomplishments. Certain of the goals have been repeatedly articulated; others are more difficult to describe. Assessing OHADA's success is yet more complicated because there is no easy measure for intangible outcomes, especially when the effects almost certainly depend on a mix of causes. An impressionistic understanding of both the goals and the accomplishments, however, can provide at least an indication of the future trajectory.

OHADA's Goals

From OHADA's inception, its purpose has been to encourage investment into the treaty territory,[1] including foreign investment, and thus to support economic development. OHADA's drafters expressly stated that intention, and anecdotal evidence reports that national governments within the territory accepted OHADA's incursion into state sovereignty because, after the regional economic downturn of the early 1990s, any support for foreign investment was welcome. In the region, the excess domestic investment compared to gross national savings was possible only

[1] See, eg, OHADA Treaty, preamble, [online] www.ohada.com; an English translation of the treaty is also available at Appendix 2.

by access to foreign sources of investment.[1] The national economies could fund the domestic investments but only by borrowing. The result, of course, is a brutal debt-to-equity ratio at the national level. Under these circumstances, any structure that promises to attract foreign direct investment becomes instantly desirable.

If, then, foreign investment is the official goal, legal professionals within the territory uniformly offer a parallel articulation of OHADA's goals, one that is of particular practical importance to the business person, by using the French phrase, 'sécurité juridique et judiciaire'. Roughly translated, it means predictability and certainty, with respect to both the interpretation and the application of the laws.

This kind of predictability, of course, is entirely compatible with the desire to attract foreign investment. Foreigners contemplating an investment in any location are always concerned about obtaining fair treatment. As distinguished from risk, uncertainty is unquantifiable. The inability to measure not only increases cost, but does so in a non-rational, unpredictable way. That is, the inability to predict may cause investors to insist on compensation for an investment that later proves to have been unnecessarily – unjustifiably – high. In its turn this reality reduces the investments' value to the host country. In the worst scenario, if investors' need for certainty leads them to pay bribes, this act will inevitably add to risk for the investors: the payment will be illegal under the laws of the host country and, increasingly, also under the laws of the payer's country of residence, which adversely affects the certainty sought from the bribe. Even without considering the cost of political corruption to the host country, potential investors thus lose; these circumstances may not dissuade all potential investors, but they do not actively encourage foreign direct investment either.

Predictability of interpretation and enforcement will not be sufficient to assure the goal of attracting foreign investment if the laws themselves are anti-commercial. Implicit is the concept that the laws themselves must be sophisticated commercial documents and well balanced between competing commercial interests. The laws, therefore, must reflect commercial values and norms. In the British tradition, this concept was familiar to the great jurist Lord Mansfield.[2] In the United States, the principal drafter of the uniform commercial law for the individual states, Karl Llewellyn, was equally certain that commercial law must track good

[1] Stein, H. (2003) Rethinking African development, in Rethinking Development Economics, ed H-J. Chang, p 153–154, Anthem Press, London (discussing foreign direct investment).

[2] Sheintag, B.L. (1941) Lord Mansfield revisited – a modern assessment, *Fordham Law Review*, 10: 345–388, p 351.

commercial practice. Thus, to promote foreign investment and development, these new laws must be predictable in their application and their application must as a practical matter further commerce.

But foreign investment is not the only game in town. While preparing a structure intended to enhance foreign investment, the OHADA drafters created a system that supports domestic investment as well. Local capital – whether classic capital or human capital – does need sophisticated commercial laws predictably interpreted and enforced. While the major international donors have historically focused on the big-impact, big-infrastructure projects, even they have now appreciated the importance of the more modest, more targeted efforts. These efforts, being smaller, are more likely to have been generated by domestic capital. This domestic investment, too, creates employment; it can even generate exports.

Implementation of OHADA's Goals

So far, OHADA has adopted eight Uniform Acts, with a ninth anticipated in 2009. These cover a wide range of commercial topics, from business organizations, to classic commercial transactions, to laws relating to workouts, and even law concerning the transport of cargo by road.[1] Because these uniform laws are the focus of OHADA, they are the locus of all tensions between OHADA and the outside. This is the case whether we look at the OHADA legislative process, its judicial process or its executive. During interviews held over the past several years, practitioners within the OHADA territory praised the Uniform Acts' sophistication and reach, and expressed deep satisfaction both about the benefits that the Uniform Acts have already generated and at their promise of more dividends brought by increased predictability. However, to consider where OHADA will go, what are the future perspectives, it is necessary first to go back in time in order to have a sense of the trajectory so far. Thus, we turn to a brief summary of the OHADA regime's search for predictability.

The legislative process

The Uniform Acts are the outcome of OHADA's legislative process. As noted above, legal professionals within the region are indeed impressed by the sophistication, structure and reach of the OHADA Uniform Acts.

[1] Available at www.ohada.com; translations of selected sections of the Uniform Acts, including all sections explicitly mentioned in the text of this book, can also be found at Appendix 4.

They consider this legislation to be well drafted on the whole, and they hope and expect that the clarity of the texts will reduce the unpredictability of judicial decisions. That is the expectation underpinning civilian codes, although even they do require interpretation, as civil law practitioners' and judges' references to scholarly commentary and other aids attest.

If the Uniform Acts are intended to reflect commercial reality within the territory, it is important that local norms in fact be reflected. This highlights the central moral issue, namely the relationship between democracy and the OHADA legislative process. Pursuant to the treaty, the OHADA legislative process is controlled by the Council of Ministers, that is, by a congress composed of representatives of the member nations' executives. Further, the Council of Ministers needs unanimous approval of at least two-thirds of its membership present and voting at a meeting to adopt a uniform act.[1] The logic is unassailable: in order to obtain the agreement of national governments to a supranational regime, these governments had to be reassured that they would have a substantial say, even a final say, in the legislation adopted. Unanimous approval obviously grants each member nation the potential to veto.

If this arrangement reassures the member states' government leaders, the regime also puts the legislative process at considerable remove from the population. Ministers of Justice or of Finance who represent their governments at the Council of Ministers are appointed, not elected. To be sure, certain of the countries within the OHADA territory have freely elected their government's executives; to that extent, the Ministers can claim democratic legitimacy at least indirectly. Further, the entire OHADA regime was typically adopted by the governments' parliaments; again, to the extent that these are democratically elected, the organs of OHADA can assert at least indirect democratic legitimacy. Functionally, however, the OHADA Council of Ministers remains a long step from the people it affects. As a practical matter, how can such an institution be confident that it understands what are the commercial norms of the people in the trenches? How can it be reasonably certain that it appreciates what new topics business people hope to see governed by Uniform Acts, and that it understands whether and to what extent the existing Acts succeed in regularizing the commercial environment?

These are the concerns that led the Permanent Secretariat and the Council of Ministers to embrace the establishment of national commissions. The original text of the treaty does not provide for these commissions, but their evolution demonstrates the flexibility and responsiveness of the

[1] OHADA Treaty, Arts. 8 & 27.

entire OHADA structure. The commissions, at their best, are the eyes and ears of the Council of Ministers. An active membership comprising practicing lawyers, judges and academics experienced in the OHADA system and its Uniform Acts propose new topics for future acts, recommend improvements to existing statutes and generally provide an interface between the formal OHADA structure and the business and legal world which it affects.

At the same time, the national commissions, because they are appointed by the relevant national government, conceptually are merely an implementation of the existing OHADA Treaty rather than an extension of OHADA's supranational reach. These commissions serve the same function as the Council of Ministers and under its direction to the extent that they engage each national government. In this way, the commissions, like the Council of Ministers that they serve, increase the likelihood that national governments will achieve unanimous approval of draft uniform acts, for example. Each government's leadership controls its commission's membership and thus can be as involved and informed as it wishes. The commissions support the essentially federal nature of OHADA, while simultaneously serving as a bridge to the commercially active population.

The evolution of national commissions remains at an early stage. Instead of formalizing these commissions by treaty, the Council of Ministers instructed an ad hoc committee to propose a form of authorizing document that each State party could adopt.[1] This choice recognizes the national commissions' importance, while leaving them the flexibility that has served them well to-date. As with all social institutions, the critical issue is how these commissions will be selected, and how they will function in practice. The more actively and professionally they seek to perform their information-gathering and network-building tasks, the more they will contribute both to OHADA's goal of predictability in commercial transactions and to the Organization's legitimacy.

Each national commission does have a particularly difficult balancing act. On one hand, it is appointed by and must answer to its national government. On the other hand, the commission is to reflect accurately and completely to its government the views of persons engaged in commerce, thus ensuring that the government of the State party possesses the relevant information when it makes its ultimate political decision to support or not the adoption of a uniform act or other text. Of course, the national government's decision controls whatever its national commission proposes, but the commission's role as conduit remains important.

---

[1] Journal Officiel no. 12, Feb. 28, 2003, pp 10, 21-25

Today, national commissions are not equally effective in all State parties. In some, they meet regularly, review drafts and propose changes. The legal professionals in those countries know who are the members of their commission and thus know to whom to address proposals concerning OHADA and its texts. The commission even solicits recommendations as to improvements. This interaction provides at least some direct, democratic input, although it is a form of weighted democracy as its members will tend to be the persons most interested in commerce and how it is effected.

Another major change currently contemplated to the OHADA structure is the formal addition of a Conference of Heads of State and of Government. While not a legislative institution, it deserves to be considered in the context of the Council of Ministers because this new Conference, if adopted, is designed to replace the Council of Ministers as the forum for expressing competing national, political concerns. As noted above, the current OHADA Treaty introduces political realities through the Council of Ministers. The proposed treaty-revisions signed in Quebec on October 17, 2008, and, as this book goes to press, circulating to complete the ratification process, recognize the political nature of the relationships among the State parties by adding the Conference, a formal institution through which the countries' executives can engage OHADA issues directly. In part, this modification reflects the reality that for many of the State parties, the executive is the most important branch.

Whether this new institution within OHADA will reinforce OHADA by offering a formal structure for a politicization that has already occurred, or whether instead it will reduce OHADA's effectiveness by politicizing an essentially commercial institution cannot be fully appreciated until it starts its work. Observation of the Council of Ministers' meetings, however, suggests that OHADA is inevitably already politically charged. An official forum for the State parties' chief executives, created to facilitate where necessary a direct and overtly political intervention, could reduce the exercise of a more indirect political influence thorough the Council of Ministers. The new Conference of Heads of State and of Government thus could allow OHADA's legislature to focus more on technical, rather than political issues.

The judicial branch

On the judicial side, implementation of the OHADA laws takes place at the point where the OHADA regime meets the national regime. Pursuant to the treaty, the OHADA laws rise to the CCJA (Common Court of Justice and Arbitration) for final interpretation, and the national governments enforce those laws.[1] This reflects further the national governments' unwillingness to shed entirely their responsibility for commercial law, even in the face of the OHADA regime's need for uniformity. And, again, the difficult moment is at the point where OHADA's laws meet the rest of the social structure.

Interpretation of the OHADA Uniform Acts may still be inconsistent to some degree from country to country and from case to case. While not immediately supportive of the laws' march towards predictability, unevenness in interpretation occurs in any judicial system. That is why judicial systems provide for appeals. In the case of the OHADA Uniform Acts, the final appeals have the added advantage of being offered in the Côte d'Ivoire, and thus in neutral territory, at least for all but Ivoirians. Further, the legal professionals both within the OHADA territory and outside it have uniformly praised the quality of the CCJA's decisions, as to both their technical sophistication and their integrity.

From the outset, national judicial systems have challenged the extent of the CCJA's appellate jurisdiction – does it apply to all cases and declaratory judgements concerning the Uniform Acts, as many believe? Or is the CCJA's jurisdiction narrower as the champions of the national supreme courts seek to maintain? This inquiry rests on a tug-of-war between the highest courts of a national judicial system and the CCJA; it will have to be resolved, of course, as it directly affects the implementation of the Uniform Acts. This type of issue is classic at the birth of any federal system; while the detail of the outcome is not yet clear, the core value of OHADA, namely the uniformity of its texts is guaranteed by the treaty, and the CCJA remains the crucial protector of that norm.

To be effective, laws not only must be sophisticated and appropriate as are OHADA's Uniform Acts, but they must in fact be enforced. Because the treaty withholds jurisdiction from the CCJA in criminal cases,[2] a critical transition point occurs here. More generally, the actual enforcement of the Uniform Acts is the responsibility of the national governments' judicial systems. Even in purely civil cases, enforcement by the various levels of national government is where the laws are most likely to lose their uniformity of impact. Disparate treatment in different national jurisdictions, and even within national jurisdictions is an unfortunate outcome not consistent with the laws' avowed purpose of creating predictability. Some differences in treatment are not surprising, of course, and various writs issued by the national judiciary, such as the writ of mandamus in the United States, are designed to address these concerns,

[1] OHADA Treaty, Art. 14.
[2] OHADA Treaty, Art. 14.

but there inevitably are serious practical issues when a member state's enforcement process is reluctant or unable to provide the final redress.

The treaty's article 14 authorizes and instructs the CCJA to interpret and assure uniform application of the treaty itself, as well as of the Uniform Acts. The treaty-revisions currently circulating for completion of the ratification process are intended to constitute a new, concededly political Conference of Heads of State and of Government as the forum for discussion of political matters, but not in any way to impinge on the CCJA's authority. Indeed, the first paragraph of article 14, as revised, explicitly increases the CCJA's jurisdiction to include not just the uniform application, but also the uniform interpretation of regulations and of the uniform acts, and of all administrative decisions of OHADA institutions as well as all judicial decisions of the national courts.[1]

The treaty-revisions further confirm the significance of the Conference by the new third paragraph to renumbered article 27(1). This paragraph stipulates that the Conference decides any and all questions concerning the treaty. As emphasized by OHADA's chief legal officer and other experts involved in the negotiations of the treaty-revisions, the intent of the new language is to provide that the CCJA decides all questions of a legal nature relating to interpretation and application of the treaty, as well as of the Uniform Acts, regulations and decisions, all as provided in revised article 14. If, however, the member states are displeased with an aspect of the treaty that is political in nature, they can address the issue through the Conference, with the sole ultimate solution being further amendment of the treaty. That is, of course, a classic configuration: the supreme judicial entity makes a decision that a political branch can subsequently modify. The political branch that has the power to overrule often is the legislature, but in the case of a supranational organization, it is reasonable that the State adhering to the treaty should be directly implicated, in this case through the Conference.

Thus, once the treaty-revisions have been fully ratified, the jurisdictional debate will be between the two most political institutions of OHADA, namely the new Conference, and the Council of Ministers. Whether we live under OHADA or merely follow it, we can only hope that the revisions, when they come into effect, will indeed be interpreted to respect the CCJA's traditional jurisdiction.

---

[1] Persons involved in the negotiations, including OHADA's chief legal officer, Mr. Idrissa Kéré, confirm that "décisions" refers to administrative decisions of all OHADA institutions as well as judicial decisions of all national courts. The revisions also add uniform interpretations of all these sources of law to the CCJA's charge of ensuring their uniform application: the revisions replace the singular "commune", that modified only "application", by the plural that modifies both interpretation and application. An English translation of the treaty-revisions currently circulating is at Appendix 3.

OHADA will have to address these issues arising at the transition between its jurisdiction and the national jurisdictions. Whether the differences across and within the OHADA territory are due to varying commercial norms, to the problem of educating the legal profession about OHADA or to other pressures including corruption, the OHADA system itself already offers support for uniform treatment. The transparency created by the presence of the CCJA and its publication of all its decisions together with a resume of the lower court decisions means that judicial activity within the territory is increasingly truly public. This facilitates identifying when properly rendered decisions are not enforced by national governments; according to local practitioners, OHADA's structure has already begun to have a salutary effect. More needs to be done, however, and ultimately all national court decisions concerning OHADA should be promptly published and distributed in order to maximize transparency, predictability and uniformity.

Indeed, members of the legal profession report that continuing efforts to distribute information within the territory about OHADA, through conferences, distribution of texts and preparation of analytic articles, are already resulting in more predictable judicial decisions, although this work is far from complete.

The executive

The Permanent Secretariat is OHADA's executive and is located in Cameroon. Despite financial strictures, the Permanent Secretariat has contributed significantly to moving OHADA from a mere concept to a living, breathing reality. As we have seen, the reality is still evolving, and the Permanent Secretariat's guidance to and support of the other OHADA organs continues to be important. For example, the role of the national commissions and their increasingly official existence is in significant part due to the Permanent Secretariat's support and general encouragement.

Especially if the member states provide the financial stability that they have promised to the OHADA institutions,[1] the Permanent Secretariat could indeed provide a unifying administrative support to the national commissions. In similar ways, it could help implement the Council of Ministers' support of transparency by further assisting in distribution of information through OHADA's special school for the purpose, ERSUMA (l'Ecole Régionale Supérieure de la Magistrature), and also by providing

[1] OHADA Treaty, Art. 43 (the treaty-revisions under consideration as this book goes to press would update this Article 43 as well); *see also Règlement No. 002-2003CM Relatif au Mécanisme de Financement Autonome de l'OHADA, Arts. 3& 4.*

technical and other support to regional universities that would be willing to organize conferences open to the practicing bar and the judiciary, as well as to law students. It is gratifying that the treaty-revisions currently circulating for ratification expressly recognize the Permanent Secretariat as OHADA's executive.

The importance of partnering with regional universities cannot be overstated. These institutions have a concentration of remarkable scholars commenting on and publicizing the OHADA uniform laws, and thus reinforcing the laws' application. In addition, on a purely practical level, universities have the capacious auditoriums that are perfect fora for bringing together large numbers of practitioners and judges at reasonable cost. The Permanent Secretariat's partnership with universities is thus critical to acceleration of the OHADA implantation not only through education of law students but also by making information easily accessible to all legal professionals.

OHADA's Future

If the trajectory of OHADA so far, then, is a commitment to uniformity and a concerted effort to enhance the effectiveness of the Uniform Acts, what can we divine about OHADA's future?

The future of OHADA within its own territory

OHADA's current evolution properly focuses on consolidating its accomplishments and continuing along the trajectory towards predictability. On the pragmatic level, at OHADA's inception the goal was to help the system evolve to the point of no return, that is, to the point from which political forces within the territory could no longer dismantle the system. The people most directly involved with OHADA within its territory are now confident that OHADA's roots are deep, although they still need to be nurtured. Lawyers and judges confirm that they are relieved to be able to locate the legal texts easily and to apply texts that carry a commercial transaction from its beginning to its end. They are pleased that the OHADA laws regularize workouts, both for a business that falls on hard times and for a specific transaction that cannot be completed because of one party's breach. The practical importance of OHADA's treatment of the end game makes sense: businesses feel the bite of law when asked to act according to promises they no longer want to keep.

The future trajectory as currently in view includes more work towards consolidation of the institutions, consideration of the transition points between OHADA and the national systems and the addition of new laws and revisions of existing ones. Consolidation of institutions is largely an issue of improving the institutions' financial backing. Although international donors have primed the pump it is important that the State parties fund the OHADA process as they had promised;[1] to confirm the importance of funding, the treaty-revisions circulating for ratification as this book goes to press focus explicitly on that topic. The effectiveness of the institutions is critically important not only within the OHADA regime but also for the transitions where the national governments become responsible for implementing the OHADA laws. If the OHADA institutions were better funded, they could do yet more to promote the laws' transparency, and the transparency of enforcement by national judicial systems. On one hand, they could accelerate the process of educating the members of each national bar and bench on the existing Uniform Acts. On the other hand, these institutions could use various modalities, including distribution of texts and commentary in hard copy and, increasingly, by Internet, to inform practitioners and judges about cases at every level of the trial and appeals process.

The institutions could also increase the information to distribute. Not only could they fund the preparation of new texts, but they could finance the collection and distribution of all cases, past and future, concerning OHADA, decided by national courts. The CCJA decisions already are systematically published, but since many decisions are not appealed to the CCJA, the national courts' pronouncements are essential components of the OHADA jurisprudence.

Proper financial support could also facilitate access to the institutions. For example, it would be helpful if the CCJA were to convince consumers of OHADA law that its physical presence only in the Côte d'Ivoire is sufficient to the purpose. Even today, the expense of travel to the Côte d'Ivoire can be limited to the actual oral arguments which, under civilian procedure, typically are not necessary and, according to informal, off-the-record comments by CCJA judges, are not even helpful. Since the written submissions are consequently very important, perhaps it would be useful if one or several offices of the CCJA were opened in each member state of the territory purely for the purpose of receiving filings. Of course, if the CCJA is not able to demonstrate convincingly that parties can equally successfully prosecute their litigation in writing, without themselves

[1] OHADA Treaty, Art. 43.

having to make a physical appearance at the CCJA, the court should propose a different structure to the State parties. The alternative will have to be both effective in the classic sense and cost-effective, no easy combination.

Moving to the legislative role of OHADA, it would be salutary if the Permanent Secretariat did become in fact a coordinator and supervisor of the national commissions on behalf of the Council of Ministers, and if the Permanent Secretariat monitored a regular procedure of interaction between those who use the OHADA laws, and the institutions that implement them. The Permanent Secretariat could, for example, support the Council of Ministers, that is, the direct representatives of the member states' governments within OHADA, in a discussion of the very practical problem of enforcement. Of course, if the Conference of Heads of State and of Government is created, that may be the better venue for settling such issues.

Even in the form of codes, law is dynamic; it is important that the Council of Ministers and, if and when available, the Conference of Heads of State and of Government, remain aware of the pressures on existing Uniform Acts. For example, there continues to be considerable excitement surrounding execution of judgements. While the high quality of expert analysis within the territory reflects a respect for the OHADA laws and a hope for their continued evolution, the issues of transition between OHADA and the member states must be addressed. The national governments inevitably will be involved in resolving these issues, and OHADA's institutions can facilitate achieving the goal of uniformity.

Also important with respect to the texts of the Uniform Acts is the issue of language. This topic is discussed in greater detail below in connection with the potential expansion of the OHADA territory, but even here it is important to note that OHADA's current State parties include four languages as official languages, namely English, French, Portuguese and Spanish, but OHADA's Treaty in its current form stipulates that French is OHADA's only working language.[1] While the treaty-revisions currently circulating for completion of the ratification process do include all four as working languages, the controlling language in the event of differences, is French. The addition of English as a working language will be a great improvement for anglophone jurists, and using a French text as the reference point is not necessarily more than an inconvenience. Nevertheless, the privileged position of French bears remembering in the larger context of language and heritage.

[1] OHADA Treaty, Art. 42.

OHADA's contribution to predictability through the legal process is important when considering the organization's future, and it already supports and is poised to enhance cross-border transactions within the OHADA territory. That entire territory is more open to all businesses based in an OHADA State party because corresponding counsel hired in the other country no longer are necessary.

OHADA can provide more; even without expanding its membership, it need not be restricted to its existing territory. As lawyers and business people in the neighbouring states become increasingly familiar with OHADA laws, trade between parties in African countries outside OHADA, and parties within the OHADA territory also will become easier and less expensive. There is, therefore, a clear reason to educate non-OHADA professionals on the OHADA laws. Furthermore, a non-OHADA lawyer or business person would be more likely to invest time in learning OHADA business laws than the laws of most non-OHADA countries because it is an investment that is useful over a large area. Under conflicts principles, for example, the parties may use the OHADA Uniform Acts as the law of the contract even if only one party is located in the OHADA territory; that may be a reasonable solution as OHADA becomes better known outside its own territory.

The future: geographic expansion of OHADA

The way to maximize the impact of OHADA is to expand the territory – an increase in members is a means of leveraging current efforts in support of OHADA and its goals. Expansion is not a necessary step: the OHADA State parties have serious work ahead of them and much that they can gain from efforts within their own territory. Nevertheless, to prepare for and contemplate the addition of new members is perfectly compatible with the current members' continuing process of implanting the OHADA judicial regime within the existing territory. The larger the OHADA territory, the greater is its positive impact. And OHADA, by the terms of its treaty, is open to all members of the African Union.[1]

But what about the French-inspired, civilian origins of OHADA and its Uniform Acts? Why should, and how could common law jurisdictions join a system that is so different in approach – and even different in language? The answer may seem facile, but it is practical.

Business is business; commerce is commerce. Whatever language the parties use, whatever legal system, the goal is commercial success, and

[1] OHADA Treaty, Art. 53.

the role of law is to create a backdrop of predictability. That is, law seeks to reassure each party that the value of the other party's promise will be preserved. Thus, while the civilian system may tend to require a breaching party to perform the promise and while a common law jurisdiction may tend to resort to monetary damages, both systems are focused on protecting the parties' expectations as of the time they entered into the contract.

Other allegedly fundamental differences between civilian-based norms and common law understandings similarly may be exaggerated as the realities play out on the African continent. The French civilian law on corporations and related business organizations may urge management to take into account the interests of constituencies other than owners far more than would the Anglo-Saxon shareholder-primacy paradigm in the North, but the divergence between the two traditions is far less obvious in Africa. It is clear neither that OHADA has adopted the broadest stakeholder paradigm from French law, nor that African States of Anglo-Saxon legal tradition have followed the United States and the United Kingdom in adopting the shareholder-primacy norm at the expense of more communitarian values. In any event, the overarching logic of business narrows any differences: even in the North, both systems recognize that owners must be able to generate a return sufficient to make their investment worth their while; otherwise, no one will provide capital.

This emphasis on similarities may seem excessively optimistic, or even naïve. For example, even if broad substantive differences are cabined by the needs of commerce, details can have a significant impact on a particular litigant or group of litigants. Any sophisticated system of business laws must help create incentives for capital owners to invest in business, but the degree to which the applicable legal regime considers shareholder rights pre-eminent may make a very real difference to an employee. And that is before we consider issues of procedure. Lawyers specialising in litigation fully appreciate that cases can be won or lost on procedural points. Thus, whatever the similarities of substantive legal principles, the niceties of procedure under different regimes can be critical to the outcome. It has been a complicated process for established legal professionals in the current OHADA territory to re-educate themselves even though the vast majority trained in legal systems based on the same French regime that informed OHADA. How much harder it may be for legal professionals trained in a common law approach. That is the most negative expression of the difficulties that common law lawyers encounter.

The introduction of common law specialists into the OHADA framework is not impossible, of course. The critical question is whether the benefits outweigh the effort to accomplish an expansion of OHADA. Based on discussions with legal professionals in the existing member states, anecdotal evidence certainly suggests that the current beneficiaries of the OHADA regime consider an extension of OHADA into, for example, neighbouring anglophone states nothing but a positive. Regional solidarity plus the prospect of easier regional trade are pro-extension motivators for legal professionals and business persons in existing State parties. Further, OHADA's anglophone neighbours boast significant commercial enterprises, making them particularly attractive adherents: a stronger OHADA can speak even more boldly to foreign investors and can generate yet more intra-territory business activity.

From the perspective of potential new members of OHADA, the calculation is a bit different. On the plus side is the powerful reality of an established, sophisticated structure, governed and used by capable and committed legal professionals. That is true for each of the non-legislative OHADA institutions: the CCJA, the Permanent Secretariat and ERSUMA. OHADA's legislative body, the Council of Ministers, is OHADA's interface with national governments and demonstrably adopts Uniform Acts unanimously approved by representatives of each member state. To join an organization that has been maturing for a decade and a half, that has been in active operation since 1998 and that already boasts 16 countries,[1] offers new entrants an enormous saving of time and energy and of financial resources. On the negative side is the fact that the OHADA territories' anglophone neighbours come from the common law tradition.

The solution is compromise. We know from other jurisdictions that it is possible for the Anglo-Saxon and civilian traditions to live side-by-side. Canada and the European Union are obvious examples, and so is Cameroon. Canada's solution is different from OHADA's, though, because unlike OHADA, the former does not apply a single uniform law to all business matters; as we have seen, the uniformity of OHADA's laws creates a substantial part of their value and thus should not be diluted. The European Union, too, is unlike OHADA because the former does not have a truly supranational legal system with uniform laws automatically adopted as the member states' internal laws.

Cameroon, with its dual legal system and with French and English as its two official languages, is in many ways the perfect test case for the inclusion of an anglophone common law country into OHADA. Cameroon has learned that with adequate advance preparation, including the early availability of conferences and texts in English, common law lawyers and judges would have experienced a far easier transition. With admirable

[1] Seventeen countries, after the Democratic Republic of Congo has completed the adoption process (the comment as of February 2009).

suppleness, members of Cameroon's anglophone bar and bench are applying the OHADA laws and are already praising their clarity and sophistication. Indeed, these jurists reserve the bulk of their criticism for the continuing issues relating to enforcement of judgements by the national governments and to language issues, namely the treaty's imposition of French as the working language and the inadequacy of currently available translations into English. Given the anglophone zone's initial reticence, this represents a very favourable report card from anglophone Cameroon. As we have already seen, the issue of enforcement depends on the will of the State parties, does not depend on OHADA or its institutions, and is precisely the same concern expressed by the OHADA territory's francophone lawyers; further, it is very much in the sights of local legal professionals, donor organizations and, to varying extent, of the national governments. The issue of language is serious and is being addressed by treaty amendment as noted above.

In all likelihood, moreover, a sovereign nation with a different legal tradition and language from that of most of the current OHADA State parties will request certain modifications to the OHADA Treaty and uniform laws as part of the negotiations when it joins. The question, of course, is how to identify those aspects of OHADA that would be open to negotiation. OHADA's characteristics critical to its success include its laws' uniformity and clarity. The advantage of a code is precisely its clarity; because the legal systems in Anglo-Saxon countries, including the United Kingdom and the United States, are increasingly statutory, the use of legislation should not shock. Uniformity, as we have seen, is central to reducing transaction costs for all investments and trades and to increasing the region's ability to negotiate with foreign investors. Thus, the statutory form of OHADA appears critical to the regime's success, but the need for statutory uniformity does not mean that content is immutable. The only way to find out what parts of the OHADA regime are open to negotiation is to start discussions. To start these discussions, OHADA and its anglophone neighbours must first address the language barrier.

There already exist a number of different translations of the OHADA texts into English, available on Web sites among other places.[1] If the new entrants are English-speaking nations, a translation of all Uniform Acts and of the treaty should be adopted by OHADA as official, whether or not the original eight Uniform Acts would retain the French texts as texts of reference. New draft Uniform Acts, in any event, should be composed from the outset in both English and French, starting immediately. Cameroon's

[1] www.ohada.com; www.juriscope.org. A ninth Uniform Act (on cooperatives) will likely be adopted in 2009; it was drafted in French.

status as a bilingual English–French member state justifies this immediate change. The addition of English as a working language will entail a substantial allocation of resources, especially since the process will – inevitably and appropriately – have to be extended to both Portuguese and Spanish due to the OHADA membership of, respectively, Guinea-Bissau and Equatorial Guinea (although French, too, is an official language for the latter).[1] Fortunately, as noted above, the treaty amendment adding these three languages is expected to be adopted very shortly.

OHADA should immediately invite their anglophone neighbours to participate on an advisory basis in discussions regarding modification of existing Uniform Acts to take into account the experience garnered over the past decade, as well as concerning adoption of new acts. Because the translation of legal texts involves concepts as well as language, the establishment of such teams is critical for the existing State parties as well as for potential future adherents. To this end, OHADA's Permanent Secretariat could assist interested legal professionals in Ghana and Nigeria, for example, to establish an unofficial national commission in each country. These unofficial commissions, together with the OHADA members' official national commissions, would create the forum to discuss the possibility of enlarging the OHADA territory. The collection of commissions would be the venue to propose substantive changes to the Uniform Acts and to consider how to handle a melding of the procedural traditions, without losing either the clarity or the uniformity that are OHADA's hallmarks.

Conclusion

OHADA has already offered its member states a clear, uniform set of business laws, with more to come. Through its institutions, it has established a sophisticated and elegant structure designed to protect the laws' uniformity. It even supports training for legal professionals within its territory. OHADA's future within that territory is assured: both the bar and the bench praise OHADA's sophistication, report that it has improved the legal climate and complain chiefly that the transition points between OHADA and the national governments still by moments compromise predictability. Such positive impact from OHADA's few years

[1] Arguably, the treaty's reference to 'working language' as opposed to 'official language' might not mandate the translation of all the texts (OHADA Treaty, Art. 42, supra note 1), but as a practical matter no anglophone country can be expected to join OHADA unless its professionals can read the applicable law.

of existence bodes very well for its future. OHADA is constructing the backdrop of legal certainty that facilitates both investment and trade.

OHADA's expansion offers significant advantages both for its existing membership and for new entrants. A larger territory offers economies of scale to the existing members, and a significant saving of time and financial resources to new members. The principal cost current and future members will experience is the compromise required to tailor the OHADA regime to anglophone countries of common law tradition. Cameroon has already demonstrated that anglophone, common law lawyers can benefit from OHADA. Importantly, however, the familiarizing of OHADA's anglophone neighbours with the Uniform Acts is its own reward as that already facilitates cross-border commercial transactions.

Those are direct commercial benefits that OHADA is already providing and will increasingly provide if its consumers and the member states' national governments help it put down firm roots. OHADA can pay important indirect dividends as well, because the very uniformity of the Uniform Acts can make it harder for a potential foreign investor to wrest specific, favourable terms from a particular country. So long as the State parties exercise the political will to ensure that the Uniform Acts are implemented in the clear and transparent fashion that OHADA contemplates and supports, the potential investor's ability to play one country off against another is reduced, to the economic advantage of all the populations of the OHADA territory.

For this reason as well, OHADA should continue to consolidate within its current territory and to embrace further discussions with OHADA's anglophone neighbours.

Appendix 1: Bibliography

Articles

Amegatcher, Andrew Ofoe (2008). The OHADA Treaty from an Anglophone Perspective. *Ghana Policy Journal, volume 2,* 111-23.

Bamodu, Gbenga (1994). Transnational Law, Unification and Harmonization of International Commercial Law in Africa. *Journal of African Law, volume 38,* 125-43.

Bourque, Jean François (2002). OHADA Four Years On: One Business Law for 16 African Countries. *International Trade Forum, volume 4.*

Bourque, Jean-François (1998). Doing Business in Sub-Saharan Africa: A Legal Revolution. *International Trade Forum, volume 3,* 22-23.

Claringbould, Maarten H. (2006). The Digital Waybill and the Digital Pen: A Success Story from the Netherlands. *Revue de Droit Uniforme, volume 9,* 667.

Clarke, Malcolm (2006). National Judges Facing Gaps in the CMR: British Case-Law. *Revue de Droit Uniforme, volume 9,* 633.

Coetzee, Juana (2006). Harmonization of Sales Law: An International and Regional Perspective. *Vindobona Journal of International Commercial Law and Arbitration, volume 10,* 15-26.

Cooper, Seward Montgomery (2004). The African Development Bank, the African Law Institute and the Harmonization of Laws in Africa. *Law for Development Bulletin 2004,* 29. OHADATA reference number: D-05-18.

Cousin, Barthélémy (2005). The Future for OHADA. OHADATA reference number: D-05-64. Available from: http://www.nortonrose.com/knowledge/publications/2005/pub11006.aspx?page=1672.

Csoklich, Peter (2006). CMR as National Law and Cabotage in Austria. *Revue de Droit Uniforme, volume 9,* 685

Date-Bah, Samuel Kofi (2004). The UNIDROIT Principles of International Commercial Contracts and the Harmonisation of the Principles of Commercial Contracts in West and Central Africa: Reflections on the OHADA Project from the Perspective of a Common Lawyer from West Africa. *Uniform Law review, volume 9,* 269-273. Available from: http://www.unidroit.org/english/publications/review/articles/2004-2-datebah-e.pdf.

Dickerson, Claire Moore (2005). Harmonizing Business Laws in Africa: OHADA Calls the Tune. *Columbia Journal of Transnational Law, volume 44,* 17-73.

Dickerson, Claire Moore (2007). The Cameroonian Experience Under OHADA: Business Organizations in a Developing Economy. *Business & Society Review, volume 112,* 2.

Djieufack, Roland (2004). The Nature of Agency Relationship Under the OHADA Uniform Act on General Commercial Law and Common Law: A Comparative Study. *Post-Graduate (maitrise) dissertation, University of Dschang.* Available from: http://www.juriscope.org/actu_juridiques/doctrine/OHADA/ohada_19.pdf.

Eisenfeld, Jamie, & François Serres (2001). African Legal Developments in the United States and Sub-Saharan Africa. *International Lawyer, volume 35,* 869-877.

Ekome, Emmanuel (2002). Public Issue of Shares Under the Companies Ordinance and the Uniform Act of the OHADA Treaty. *Juris Périodique, volume 50,* 95-108.

Enonchong, Nelson E. (2002). The Harmonization of Business Law in Africa: Is Article 42 of the OHADA Treaty a Problem? *Journal of African Law, volume 51:1,* 95-116.

Ferrari, Franco (2001). International Sales Law in the Light of the OHBLA Uniform Act Relating To General Commercial Law and the 1980 Vienna Sales Convention. *Revue de Droit des Affaires Internationales, volume 5,* 599.

Ferrari, Franco (2001). The OHBLA Draft Uniform Act on Contracts for the Carriage of Goods By Road. *Revue de Droit des Affaires Internationales, volume 7,* 798.

Fontaine, Marcel (2004). The Draft OHADA Uniform Act on Contracts and the UNIDROIT Principles of International Commercial Contracts. *Uniform Law Review, volume 9,* 573-584. OHADATA reference number: D-05-02. Available from: http://www.unidroit.org/english/publications/review/articles/2004-3-fontaine-e.pdf.

Forneris, Xavier (2001). Harmonising Commercial Law in Africa: The OHADA. *Juris Périodique, volume 46,* 77-85. OHADATA reference number: D-05-21.

Forneris, Xavier (2001). Harmonizing Commercial Law in Africa: The OHADA. *Juris Périodique, volume 46,* 77-85.

Kenfack, Gaston Douajni (2003). The Recognition and Enforcement of Arbitral Awards in OHADA Member States. *Journal of International Arbitration, volume 20,* 205-210.

Lecerf, M., et. al. (1999). The Arbitration in the Treaty for the Harmonisation of African Business Law (OHADA): A New Common Law for Institutional Arbitration. *International Construction Law Review, volume 16(2),* 287-293.

Mancuso, Salvatore (2007). Trends on the Harmonization of Contract Law in Africa. *Annual Survey of International and Comparative Law, volume 13,* 157-178.

Mancuso, Salvatore (2008). The New African Law: Beyond the Difference Between Common Law and Civil Law. *Annual Survey of International and Comparative Law, volume 14,* 39-60.

Martor, Boris and Thouvenot, Sébastien (2004). Business Law in Africa: OHADA – Harmonisation Supports Africa's Development. *International Highlights, the Law Society, volume 17.* OHADATA reference number: D-04-20.

Martor, Boris and Thouvenot, Sébastien. The OHADA Legal Harmonisation Process: The Benefits for Africa's Development. OHADATA reference number: D-04-22.

Mbifi, Richard. Reflecting on OHADA Law Reform Mission: Its Impact on Certain Aspects of Company Law in Anglophone Cameroon. OHADATA reference number: D-04-42.

Muna, Akere (2001). Is OHADA Common Law Friendly? *International Law Forum du droit international, volume 3,*172-179.

Nah, Thomas Fuashi. (2002). Pre-Incorporation Contracts and the Impossibility of Ratification Under Common Law – the Salutary Jettison of a Stifling Principle by the Civil Law Inspired Uniform Act Relating to Commercial Companies and Economic Interest Groups Enacted by OHADA. *Annales de la Faculté de Droit de Dschang, 2002,* 69. OHADATA reference number: D-04-40.

Nyambo, Temngah Joseph. (2001). The Legal System of Trial in Cameroon: Implementing the OHADA Treaty in Anglophone Cameroon. *Juris Périodique, volume 47,* 100-05.

Penda, Jean Alain and Tumnde, Martha Simo. Problems of Implementation of OHADA in Anglophone Cameroon. OHADATA reference number: D-04-13.

Penda, Jean Alain and Tumnde, Martha Simo. The Roadmap of the Harmonization of Business Law in Africa. OHADATA reference number: D-04-14.

Penda, Jean Alain. OHADA and the Era of Globalization. OHADATA reference number: D-04-16.

Tabe Tabe, Simon. (2002). Some Antipodal Hurdles that Beset the Uniform Working of the OHADA Uniform Acts in Cameroon. *Annales de la Faculté de Droit de Dschang, 2002,* 33. OHADATA reference number: D-04-38.

Thouvenot, Sébastien and Martor, Boris. (2004). Business Law in Africa: OHADA – Harmonisation Supports Africa's Development. *International Highlights, the Law Society, volume 17.* OHADATA reference number: D-04-20.

Thouvenot, Sébastien and Martor, Boris. The OHADA Legal Harmonisation Process: The Benefits for Africa's Development. OHADATA reference number: D-04-22.

Touray, Sharif A. The OHADA Treaty: Recent Developments Will Spur African Investment and Project Financings. 1999. Available from: http://library.findlaw.com/1999/Jul/1/130357.html

Tuma, Otmar J. (2006). The Degree of Default Under Article 29 CMR. *Revue de Droit Uniforme, volume 9,* 585.

Tumnde, Martha Simo (2002). Government Control and Supervision of insurance Companies in Cameroon: An Appraisal of the CIMA Code. *Annales de la Faculté de Droit de Dschang, 2002,* 141. OHADATA reference number: D-04-44.

Tumnde, Martha Simo (2002). The Applicability of the OHADA Treaty in Cameroon. Annales de la Faculté de Droit de Dschang, 2002, 23. OHADATA reference number: D-04-37.

Tumnde, Martha Simo (2002). The Premise, the Promise and the Problem of the CIMA Code in Cameroon. *Annales de la Faculté de Droit de Dschang, 2002,* 121. OHADATA reference number: D-04-43.

Tumnde, Martha Simo and Penda, Jean Alain. Problems of Implementation of OHADA in Anglophone Cameroon. OHADATA reference number: D-04-13.

Tumnde, Martha Simo and Penda, Jean Alain. The Roadmap of the Harmonization of Business Law in Africa. OHADATA reference number: D-04-14.

Yakubu, John Ademola. Debt Recovery Procedures and Enforcement Measures: OHADA Approach and the Approach of Common Aw - Which Is Better? OHADATA reference number: D-04-27.

Studies

World Bank (2009) *Doing Business – OHADA*, available at http://www.doingbusiness.org/Documents/RegionalReports/DB09_Organization_Harmonization_Business_Law_Africa.pdf (last visited Sept. 19, 2008)

Books

Asouzu, Amazu A. (2001). International Commercial Arbitration and African States: Practice, Participation and Institutional Development. Cambridge: Cambridge University Press.

I.B.P.–U.S.A. (2008). Harmonization of Business Law in Africa (OHADA) Handbook (6th edition). Washington, DC: International Business Publications, USA.

Idris, Mohammed Baba, ed. (2007). Harmonization of Business Law in Africa: The Law, Issues, Problems and Prospects. Lagos: Corporate Legal Consulting.

Larson, Fred R., et al. (2002). Business Law in Africa: OHADA and the Harmonization Process. London: Kogan Page, Limited.

Mator, Boris, et al. (2007). Business Law In Africa: OHADA and the Harmonisation Process (2nd edition). London: GMB Publishing Limited.

Websites

www.ohada.org
This is the official OHADA website but is still under construction.

www.ohada.com
Built and maintained by UNIDA, a non-government organization whose founding president was Judge Kéba MBAYE, former Vice President of the International Court of Justice in The Hague and former justice of the Supreme Court of Senegal, and whose current president is Judge Seydou BA, formerly the inaugural President of OHADA's Common Court of Justice and Arbitration. In addition to general information about OHADA, the website contains a translation into English of the Treaty and the Uniform Acts, as well as a substantial collection of English-language articles.

www.juriscope.org
This site was founded by and is under the direction of Professor Jacques DAVID, an renowned specialist in comparative law. This site contains a translation of the OHADA Treaty and of the Uniform Acts. As this book goes to press, it also offers an annotated translation into English of three Uniform Acts; more are in production

Appendix 2

Treaty on the Harmonization of Business Law in Africa

(Original Treaty 1993 - English Translation)[1]

PREAMBLE

The President of THE REPUBLIC OF BENIN
The President of BURKINA FASO
The President of THE CAMEROON REPUBLIC
The President of CENTRAL AFRICAN REPUBLIC
The President of ISLAMIC FEDERAL REPUBLIC OF THE COMOROS
The President of THE CONGO REPUBLIC
The President of IVORY COAST REPUBLIC
The President of GABONESE REPUBLIC
The President of EQUATORIAL GUINEA REPUBLIC
The President of MALI
The President of NIGER
The President of SENEGAL
The President of CHAD
The President of TOGO.

HIGH CONTRACTING AUTHORITIES TO THE TREATY ON THE HARMONIZATION OF BUSINESS LAW IN AFRICA.
Determined to accomplish new progress on the road to African unity and to establish a feeling of trust in favour of the economies of the Contracting States in a view to create a new centre of development in Africa;

Reaffirming their commitment in favour of the establishment of an African Economic Community;

Convinced of the fact that their membership in the franc zone is an economic and monetary stability factor and constitutes a major asset for the progressive

[1] Unoffical translation, as available at www.juriscope.org and www.ohada.com, except that "OHBLA" has been replaced by "OHADA".

realisation of their economic integration and that this integration must be carried on in a larger African framework;

Mindful of the fact that the realisation of those objectives demands an application in the Contracting States of a business law which is simple, modern and adaptable;

Conscious of the fact that it is essential that this law be applied with diligence in such conditions so as to guarantee legal stability of economic activities and to favour expansion of the latter and to encourage investment;

Desiring to promote arbitration as an instrument to settle contractual disputes;

Determined to participate in common new efforts to better the training of Judges and Representatives of the law.

Have agreed as follows

TITLE I: GENERAL CLAUSES

Article 1: The objective of the present Treaty is the harmonisation of business laws in the Contracting States by the elaboration and adoption of simple modern common rules adapted to their economies, by setting up appropriate judicial procedures, and by encouraging arbitration for the settlement of contractual disputes.

Article 2: So as to implement the present Treaty, it is to be understood by Business Law regulations concerning Company Law, definition and classification of legal persons engaged in trade, proceeding in respect credits and recovery of debts, means of enforcement, bankruptcy, receiverships, arbitration; are also included the following laws: Employment law, Accounting law, Transportation and Sales laws, and any such other matter that the Council of Ministers would decide, unanimously, to so include as falling within the definition of Business Law, in conformity with the objective of the present Treaty and of the provisions of Article 8.

Article 3: The realisation of the tasks planned in the present Treaty shall be implemented by an organisation called the Organisation for the Harmonisation of Business Law in Africa (OHADA), consisting of a Council of Ministers and a Common Court of Justice and Arbitration.

The Council of Ministers shall be assisted by a Permanent Secretary Office to which is attached a Regional High Judiciary School.

Article 4: Regulations for the implementation of the present Treaty will be laid down if necessary by an overall majority of the Council of Ministers.

TITLE II: THE UNIFORM ACTS

Article 5: Acts enacted for the adoption of common rules as provided for in Article 1 of the present Treaty are to be known as «Uniform Acts».

Uniform Acts may include provisions to give rise to criminal liabilities.

Contracting States commit themselves to enforce sentences of offences.

Article 6: Uniform Acts are to be prepared by the Permanent Secretary Office in consultation with the Governments of Contracting States. They are to be debated and adopted by the Council of Ministers on consultation with the Common Court of Justice and Arbitration.

Article 7: Draft versions of Uniform Acts are to be issued by the Permanent Secretary Office to the Governments of Contracting States, who will have ninety days from the date of reception of the draft versions to submit their written observations to the Permanent Secretary Office.

After expiration of the ninety days delay period, the draft versions of the Uniform Acts, supplemented with observations of the Contracting States and together with a Report from the Permanent Secretary Office, is to be immediately forwarded to the Common Court of Justice and Arbitration. The Court will declare its opinion thereof within thirty days of its receipt of a request for consultation.

At the expiration of this consultation period, the Permanent Secretary Office will finalise the text of the draft versions for the Uniform Acts, and ask that it be listed on the agenda of the next Council of Minister's meeting.

Article 8: Adoption of the Uniform Acts by the Council of Ministers requires unanimous approval of the representatives of the Contracting States who are present and who have exercised their right to vote.

For such adoption of the Uniform Acts to be valid, at least two-thirds of the Contracting States shall be represented.

Abstention does not delay adoption of the Uniform Acts.

Article 9: The Uniform Acts come into force ninety days after their adoption, except with regard to particular clauses exempted there from by the Uniform Acts themselves. They may be opposed within thirty days after their publication in the Official Journal of OHADA. The Acts are also to be published in the official publications of the Contracting States or by any other appropriate means.

Article 10: Uniform Acts are directly applicable and overriding in the Contracting States notwithstanding any conflict they may give rise to in respect of previous or subsequent enactment of municipal laws.

Article 11: The Council of Ministers, upon recommendation on behalf of the Permanent Secretary Office, approves the annual program for the harmonisation of Business laws.

Article 12: Uniform Acts can only be modified under the conditions provided in Articles 7 to 9, at the request of any Contracting State.

TITLE III: LITIGATION CONCERNING INTERPRETATION AND ENFORCEMENT OF THE UNIFORM ACTS

Article 13: Litigation regarding the implementation of Uniform Acts is settled in the first instance and on appeal within the courts and tribunals of the Contracting States.

Article 14: The Common Court of Justice and Arbitration will rule on, in the Contracting States, the interpretation and enforcement of the present Treaty, on such Regulations as laid down for their application, and on the Uniform Acts.

The Court may be consulted by any Contracting State or by the Council of Ministers on all questions falling within the field of the preceding paragraph. The right to request the advice of the Court, as herein before mentioned, is recognised to the national courts hearing a case where Article 13 applies.

By way of appeal, the Court shall rule on the decisions pronounced by the appellate courts of Contracting States in all business issues raising questions pertaining to the application of Uniform Acts and to the Regulations provided for in the present Treaty, save decisions regarding penal sanctions pronounced by the appellate courts.

The Court will rule as above with regard to non-appeallable decisions delivered by any national court of the Contracting States which pertains to those matters brought to the attention of the Court by virtue of the above paragraphs.

While sitting as a court of final appeal, the Court can hear and decide points of fact.

Article 15: Final appeals, as provided in Article 14, are brought to the Common Court of Justice and Arbitration, either directly by one of the parties to the proceedings or by referral of a national court ruling on appeal, on a case to which it is referred and which raises questions concerning the application of the Uniform Acts.

Article 16: The hearing of a case on appeal by the Court, stays automatically all proceedings in view of instituting an appeal before a national court against the decision in question. However this rule does not interfere with the execution of proceedings.

Such proceedings can only be carried out after that a decision of the Common Court of Justice and Arbitration declares itself as lacking jurisdiction to hear the matter in question.

Article 17: Manifest lack of jurisdiction of the Common Court of Justice and Arbitration Court may be raised proprio motu and by all parties to the litigation in limine litis. The Court shall reach a decision within thirty days.

Article 18: Any party who, having raised before a national court hearing an appeal from inferior courts, that that national court lacks jurisdiction by virtue of the powers of the Common Court of Justice and Arbitration in the course of hearing the same appeal, can thereafter appeal to the Common Court of Justice and Arbitration within two months of the issue of the pronouncement of the contested determination.

The Court decides matters of jurisdiction on a ruling which it brings to the attention of the parties, as well as to such national court which is involved.

If the Court finds that such a national court has wrongly declared itself competent in determining an issue, the Court shall declare that latter determination as ultra vires and quashed.

Article 19: The procedure before the Common Court of Justice and Arbitration is to be laid down by Regulations adopted by the Council of Ministers pursuant to the provisions as set out in Article 8 and shall be published in the official publication of the OHADA, as well as in the official publications of the Contracting States, or, as the case may be, in or by any other appropriate means.

Proceedings shall be adversarial in nature. Each party must be represented by a duly qualified lawyer. The hearing shall be held in public.

Article 20: The judgements of the Common Court of Justice and Arbitration are final and conclusive. Execution and enforcement shall be ensured by the Contracting States on their respective territories. In no case may a decision contrary to a judgement of the Common Court of Justice and Arbitration be lawfully executed in a territory of a Contracting State.

TITLE IV: ARBITRATION

Article 21: In applying a arbitration clause or an out of court settlement, any party to a contract may, either because it has its domicile or its usual residence in one of the Contracting States, or if the contract is enforced or to be enforced in its entirety or partially on the territory of one or several contracting States, refer a contract litigation to the arbitration procedure provided in this section.

The Common Court of Justice and Arbitration does not itself settle such disagreements. It shall name and confirm the arbitrators, be informed of the progress of the proceedings, and examine decisions, in accordance with Article 24.

Article 22: Disagreements may be settled by one arbitrator or by three arbitrators. In this and the following articles, the expression «the arbitrator» means either one or more arbitrators.

When the parties have agreed that the disagreement will be settled by only one arbitrator, they may appoint him under a mutual agreement subject to approval of the Court. If there is any disagreement between the parties, an arbitrator shall be appointed by the Court within thirty days from the date of notification from one party to another to have recourse to arbitration.

Where three arbitrators are to hear a matter, each party - pursuant to a request for an arbitrator and in view to comply to such a request - shall appoint an independent arbitrator, such appointment being subject to the approval of the Court. If one of the parties refuses or cannot do so, the Court shall appoint an arbitrator on behalf of that party. A third arbitrator, shall also be appointed solely by the Court and who will sit as Chairman. The Court may however allow the choice of the third arbitrator to be made by the two other arbitrators only where there the latter have given an undertaking that they would elect as between them a third one, and this within a given period. In such a case, it is to the Court to approve the third arbitrator. If, at the expiration of the period fixed by the parties or allowed by the Court, the arbitrators cannot reach an agreement between themselves, the third arbitrator shall be chosen and appointed by the Court.

If the parties have not agreed upon the number of arbitrators, the Court shall appoint one sole arbitrator, unless it appears to the Court that the case must be tried by three arbitrators. In such a case, each party shall have fifteen days to appoint an arbitrator.

The arbitrators may be chosen from the list of arbitrators established by the Court and updated annually. Members of the Court cannot be registered on that list.

The Court may rule on any challenge of an arbitrator by any prty.

An Arbitrator shall be replaced in such circumstances as hereinafter set out, namely, where he or she has passed away, he or she is unable to perform his or her duties, he or she is to resign from office whether by reason of a challenge as to his or her suitability or otherwise, and where the Court, after enquiry decides that he or she has not fulfilled his or her obligations according to such rules of arbitration as may be applicable and according to this Treaty, or within such time as has been specified in relation to any matter. In any case, the proceedings must with paragraphs two and three of this article.

Article 23: Any national court of a Contracting State hearing a case wherein the parties have agreed that the matter to be resolved by arbitration shall hold itself as lacking jurisdiction to hear the case and, if necessary, refer the matter to Arbitration Proceedings.

Article 24: Before signing a partial or final award, the arbitrator shall submit the proposed decision to the Common Court of Justice and Arbitration, which may suggest any formal amendments to such a decision.

Article 25: Award pronounced in compliance with the stipulations provided herein shall have final and conclusive authorities in the territory of each Contracting State as judgements delivered by their national courts.

Such decisions may be enforced and executed by an order of Exequatur.

Only the Common Court of Justice and Arbitration has jurisdiction to pronounce an order of Exequatur.

Exequatur may not be issued in the following cases:

1. The Arbitrator has not ruled by virtue of an agreement giving him jurisdiction, or has ruled by virtue of a void or expired agreement
2. The Arbitrator has not ruled in compliance with its conferred mandate.
3. The principle of adversarial procedure has not been respected.
4. The decision is contrary to international public order.

Article 26: The Arbitration Regulations of the Common Court Justice and Arbitration Court shall be laid down by the Council of Ministers under the conditions provided for in Article 8. They shall be published in the Official Journal of the OHADA, and shall also be published in the official publications of the Contracting States and in or by any other appropriate means.

TITLE V: THE INSTITUTIONS

Article 27: The Council of Ministers shall consist of the Ministers responsible for Justice and Ministers responsible for Finance.

The chair of the Council shall be vested in turn by each Contracting State for a duration of a year, in the following order:

Benin, Burkina Faso, Cameroon, Central African Republic, Comoros, Congo, Ivory Coast, Gabon, Equatorial Guinea, Mali, Niger, Senegal, Chad (Tchad), and Togo.

Where a Contracting State cannot assume the chair of the Council of Ministers during such a year in which it has to do so, the Council shall appoint the chair to the next Contracting State according to the order provided as above.

Article 28: The Council of Ministers shall meet at least once a year upon notification from the Chairman, such notification being issued on his initiative or on the initiative of a third of the Contracting Parties. No deliberation shall take place unless at least two-thirds of the Contracting States are represented.

Article 29: The Chairman of the Council of Ministers set the agenda upon proposals from the Permanent Secretary Office.

Article 30: The decisions of the Council of Ministers, other than those provided in Article 8, are reached by an overall majority of the Contracting States present and voting. Each State can cast only one vote.

Article 31: The Common Court of Justice and Arbitration shall consist of seven Judges elected for seven years and re-eligible once, from among the nationals of the Contracting States, in the following functions and under the following conditions:

1. Judges having acquired a judicial experience of at least fifteen years and having exercised high judicial functions.
2. Barristers who are members of the Bar of one of the contracting States and who have at least fifteen years standing.
3. Law Professors having at least fifteen years of professional experience.

Only two members of the Court may belong to the categories referred to in paragraphs 2 and 3 above.

One seventh of the Court is renewed each year. The Court shall not consist of more than one national of the same State.

Article 32: The members of the Court are elected by secret ballot by the Council of Ministers from a roll of nominated candidate presented for this purpose by the Contracting States.

Every State may nominate two or more candidates.

Article 33: The Permanent Secretary Office shall invite the Contracting States to proceed, within a period of at least four months before the elections, with the nomination of candidates to the Court.

The Permanent Secretary Office shall establish an alphabetical roll of the nominated candidates and shall provide a copy thereof to the Contracting States at least one month before the polling date.

Article 34: After their election, the members of the Court shall solemnly take oath to undertake faithfully their functions in full impartiality.

Article 35: In the event of death of a member of the Court, the President of the Court immediately informs the Permanent Secretary Office thereof and the Permanent Secretary Office declares the seat vacant since the date of death.

In case of the resignation of a member of the Court, or if, with the unanimous consent of the other members of the Court, a member has ceased to fulfil his functions for any other reason other than of a temporary nature, or is no more capable of fulfilling them, the President of the Court, after having invited the concerned member to appear before the Court and to give his oral submissions, shall inform the Permanent Secretary Office who shall declare the seat vacant.

In each of the above circumstances, the Council of Ministers shall proceed under the conditions of Articles 32 and 33, for the replacement of the member whose seat become vacant, for the period of the mandate still to be carried on, except if six months or less remain in the mandate.

Article 36: The members of the Court shall have the security of tenure.

All members of the Court shall remain in duty until the date when his successor takes up his office.

Article 37: The Court shall elect among its own members, for a duration of three years and a half non renewable, its President and two Vice Presidents. The members of the Court whose mandate length is still running at the date of the election and is less than this duration, may be elected to exercise those functions until the expiration of their mandate. They can be reappointed to those functions if they are elected by the Council of Ministers to exercise a new mandate as member of the Court.

No member of the Court shall exercise political or administrative functions.

All remunerated activities must be authorised by the Court.

Article 38: The duration of the mandate of the seven Judges nominated simultaneously for the initial constitution of the Court will be respectively for three years, five years, six years, seven years, eight years and nine years. The mandate for each Judge will be determined by drawing lots, executed by the President of the Council of Ministers, during a session of the Council of Ministers. The first renewal of the Court will take place three years from the date of its initial constitution.

Article 39: The President of the Common Court of Justice and Arbitration shall appoint the chief Registrar of the Court on advice of the Court, from among the chief Registrars of at least fifteen years standing, and presented by the member States.

Upon proposal of the chief Registrar, the President shall fix, the other offices of the Court.

The chief Registrar is in charge of the Registrar office of the Court.

Article 40: The Permanent Secretary shall be appointed by the Council of Ministers for a four years term of office, renewable once.

He shall appoint his staffs in compliance with the conditions for the recruitment laid down by the council of Ministers and within the fixed number the staffs provided in the budget.

He shall be in charge of the Permanent Secretary Office.

Article 41: A Regional High Judiciary School shall contribute to the training and improvement of the Judges and judiciary staff of the contracting States.

The Director of the School shall be appointed by the Council of Ministers.

The organisation, management, resources and the services of the School will be defined by a regulation of the Council of Ministers laid down upon the report of the school Director.

Article 42: French shall be the working language of OHADA.

TITLE VI: FINANCIAL PROVISIONS

Article 43: The resources of the OHADA consist principally of:

(*a*) The annual contribution of the contracting States,
(*b*) The loans concluded in conventions signed by OHADA with States or international organisations,
(*c*) Gifts and legacies.

The sum of the contributions of the contracting States is fixed by the Council of Ministers. The Council of Ministers shall approve the conventions referred to in paragraph (b) and accepts the gifts and legacies referred to in paragraph (c).

Article 44: Costs rate for the arbitration proceedings provided by the present Treaty as well as the distribution of the corresponding receipts shall be approved by the Council of Ministers.

Article 45: The annual budgets of the Common Court of Justice and Arbitration and of the Permanent Secretariat shall be approved by the Council of Ministers. The accounts for each accounting period shall be certified by commissaries of accounts appointed by the Council of Ministers. They shall be approved by the Council of Ministers.

TITLE VII: STATUS, IMMUNITIES AND PRIVILEGES

Article 46: The OHADA has full international judicial personality. It has in particular the capacity:

(*a*) to contract;
(*b*) to acquire furniture and real estate and to transfer them; and
(*c*) to initiate legal proceedings and to be a party in litigation's

Article 47: So as to fulfil its duties properly, the OHADA shall possess on the territories of each contracting State immunities and privileges provided in the present title.

Article 48: The assets and possessions of the OHADA shall not be subject to any judicial action, except if it renounces to its immunity.

Article 49: The civil servants and employees of the Permanent Secretariat Office, the Regional High Judiciary School and the Common Justice and Arbitration Court, as well as the Judges of the Court and the Arbitrators designated by the latter, shall possess privileges and diplomatic immunities during the exercise of their functions. Furthermore, the Judges shall not, without due authorisation of the Court, be prosecuted for acts accomplished outside their official capacities.

Article 50: Nobody shall have access to the archives of OHADA wherever they are.

Article 51: OHADA, its properties, possessions and revenues as well as the operations authorised by the present Treaty are exonerated from all taxes and custom duties. The OHADA is also exempt from any obligation related to the recovery or payment of taxes or custom duties.

TITLE VIII: PROTOCOL CLAUSES

Article 52: The present Treaty shall be ratifies by the signatory States in accordance with their respective constitutional processes.

The present Treaty shall come into force sixty days after the date of deposit of the seventh instrument of ratification. However, if the date of the deposit of the seventh instrument of ratification is earlier than the hundred eightieth day that follows the day of signature of the Treaty, the Treaty will be enforceable the two hundred fortieth day following the day of its signature.

With regard to any contracting State which shall deposit later its instrument of ratification, the Treaty and the Uniform Acts adopted before the ratification will be enforceable sixty days after the date of the aforesaid deposit.

Article 53: The present Treaty, as soon as it becomes enforceable, is open to all members of the O.A.U. not signatory of the Treaty. It is equally open to the adhesion of any other State not member of the O.A.U. invited to adhere to it, upon unanimous agreement of all contracting States.

With regard to any contracting State, the present Treaty and the Uniform Acts approved before its admission shall come into force sixty days after the deposit of the instrument of admission.

Article 54: No reserve is allowed to the present Treaty.

Article 55: As soon as the Treaty comes into force, the common institutions provided in Articles 27 to 41 will be established. Signatory States which have not yet ratified it may moreover sit at the Council of Ministers in the capacity of observers without right to vote.

Article 56: Any dispute that may arise between contracting States regarding the interpretation or the application of the present Treaty and which would not be settled amiably may be referred by a contracting State to the Common Court of Justice and Arbitration.

If a Judge of the nationality of one of the parties is sitting in the Court, any other party may appoint an ad hoc Judge to sit for the hearing of the case.

This last one will have to fill the conditions provided in Article 31.

Article 57: The instruments of ratification and the instruments of adhesion will be filed with the Government of Senegal which will be the authorised depository Government.

Article 58: Any State ratifying the present Treaty or adhering to it after an amendment to the present Treaty has become enforceable shall be deemed to be a party to the Treaty as amended.

The Council of Ministers adds the name of the adherent State on the list provided by Article 27, preceding immediately the name of the State which assumes the presidency at the date of the admission.

Article 59: The depository Government shall register the Treaty to the Secretary of the O.A.U. and to the United Nations Secretary Office in accordance with Article 102 of the United Nations Charter.

Article 60: The depository Government will inform without delay all the signatory or adherent States of:

(*a*) the dates of signatures
(*b*) the registration dates to the Treaty
(*c*) the filing dates of the instruments of ratification and adhesion.
(*d*) the date of the coming into effect of the Treaty.

TITLE IX: REVISION AND DENUNCIATION

Article 61: The present Treaty may be amended or revised if a contracting State sends to that effect a written request to the Permanent Secretary Office of OHADA. The amendment or the revision must be adopted in the same form as the Treaty.

Article 62: The present Treaty has an unlimited duration. In any event it shall not be denounced ten years before its coming into effect.

Any denunciation of the present Treaty must be notified to the depository Government and will take effect only one year after the date of such notification.

Article 63: The present Treaty, written in two copies in the French language, will be deposited in the archives of the Republic of Senegal which shall deliver a certified true copy to each Government of the contracting States.

In witness thereof, the Head of States and plenipotentiaries undersigned have affixed their signatures at the end of the present Treaty.

Executed in Port-Louis, Mauritius, on 7th October 1993.

Appendix 3

2008 Revisions to the Treaty on the Harmonization of Business Law in Africa

(English Translation[1])

Revising the Treaty on the Harmonization of Business Law in Africa, signed at Port-Louis, Mauritius, October 17, 1993

PREAMBLE

The President of the Republic of Benin
The President of Burkina Faso
The President of the Republic of Cameroon
The President of the Central African Republic
The President of the Union of Comoros
The President of the Republic of Congo
The President of the Republic of Côte d'Ivoire
The President of the Republic of Gabon
The President of the Republic of Guinea
The President of the Republic of Guinea Bissau
The President of the Republic of Equatorial Guinea
The President of the Republic of Mali
The President of the Republic of Niger
The President of the Republic of Senegal
The President of the Republic of Chad
The President of the Republic of Togo

THE HIGH CONTRACTING PARTIES OF THE TREATY,

Reaffirm their determination to make new progress towards African unity, and their desire to reinforce legal and judicial security in the territory of the Organization for the Harmonization in Africa of Business Law (OHADA), in order to guarantee a climate of trust that will contribute to making Africa a center of development;

Determined to use the harmonization of business law as an instrument to reinforce the rule of law, as well as legal and economic integration;

---

[1] Unoffical translation prepared by Claire Moore Dickerson and Jean Alain Penda Matipé

Resolved to create all conditions necessary to consolidate the accomplishments of OHADA, and to enhance and promote them;

Agree to modify, amend and complete the Treaty on the harmonization of business law in Africa, signed at Port-Louis (Mauritius) October 17, 1993:

ARTICLE 1

Articles 3, 4, 7, 9, 12, 14, 17, 27, 31, 39, 40, 41, 42, 43, 45, 49, 57, 59, 61 and 63 of the Treaty on harmonization of business law in Africa, signed at Port Louis (Mauritius) on October 17, 1993, are modified, amended and completed as follows:

Article 3: An organization named Organization for the Harmonization in Africa of Business Law (OHADA) is responsible for effecting the tasks contemplated by the present Treaty.

OHADA includes the Conference of Heads of State and of Government, the Council of Ministers, the Common Court of Justice and Arbitration, and the Permanent Secretariat.

The headquarters (official seat) of OHADA is located in Yaounde in the Republic of Cameroon. It can be transferred to any other location by a decision of the Conference of Heads of State and of Government.

Article 4: Whenever necessary, the Council of Ministers shall, by an absolute majority, adopt regulations for the application of the present Treaty and take other actions.

Article 7: The Permanent Secretariat shall provide drafts of the Uniform Acts to the Governments of the Contracting Parties, which shall then have ninety days, starting on the date of receipt of such drafts, to deliver their written comments to the Permanent Secretariat.

Considering the circumstances, including the complexity of the text to be adopted, such ninety-day period may be extended for another ninety days upon the Permanent Secretariat's request.

At the expiration of the period including any extension, the Permanent Secretariat shall immediately forward to the Common Court of Justice and Arbitration for its advice the draft Uniform Act, together with the Contracting Parties' comments and a report of the Permanent Secretariat. The Court shall provide its advice within sixty days after receipt of such request from the Permanent Secretariat.

Upon the expiration of this last period, the Permanent Secretariat shall complete the final text of the draft Uniform Act, and shall propose it for inclusion in the agenda of the Council of Ministers' next following meeting.

Article 9: Within sixty days after their adoption, the Permanent Secretariat shall cause the Uniform Acts to be published in the Official Journal of OHADA. The

Uniform Acts become effective ninety days after such publication, unless these Uniform Acts contain different preconditions to entry into force.

The Uniform Acts are also published in the Contracting Parties, in their Official Journals or by any other appropriate means. This formality does not affect the Uniform Acts' entry into force.

Article 12: At the request of any Contracting Party or of the Permanent Secretariat, and upon authorization of the Council of Ministers, the Uniform Acts may be modified.

The modification is effected in accordance with the conditions set out in Articles 6 through 9, above.

Article 14: The Common Court of Justice and Arbitration is responsible for the uniform interpretation and uniform application of the Treaty, of the regulations promulgated to further the Treaty's implementation, of the Uniform Acts, and of other actions.

The Court may be consulted by any Contracting Party, or by the Council of Ministers, on any question within the scope of the prior paragraph. The same ability to request consultative advice from the Court shall belong to national courts hearing a case pursuant to Article 13, above.

On appeal, the Court shall rule on decisions rendered by appellate courts of the Contracting Parties with respect to all matters raising issues relative to the application of the uniform acts and the regulations contemplated by the Treaty, except for decisions applying criminal sanctions.

The Court shall rule in the same manner on non-appealable decisions rendered in the same litigation by any court of the Contracting Parties.

When sitting as a court of final appeal, the Court shall decide on the merits.

Article 17: In the event that it manifestly lacks competence in a matter, the Common Court of Justice and Arbitration may raise the issue sua sponte, as may, before trial, any party to the litigation.

The Court shall decide within thirty days following receipt of comments from the adverse party, or within thirty days following the expiration of the time allowed for the submission of said comments.

Article 27:

1. The Conference of Heads of State and of Government is composed of Heads of State and of Government of the Contracting Parties. The Conference is chaired by the Head of State or of Government whose country chairs the Council of Ministers.

The Conference shall meet when necessary. It shall be convened by its Chair, upon call by the Chair or by one-third of the Contracting Parties.

The Conference decides any and all questions concerning the Treaty.

There is a quorum for decisions of the Conference only if at least two-thirds of the Contracting Parties are present.

Actions of the Conference are effective only if adopted by consensus or, failing that, by an absolute majority of the Contracting Parties present at the meeting.

2. The Council of Ministers is composed of the Contracting Parties' Ministers of Justice and Ministers of Finance.

   The Council of Ministers shall be chaired by the Contracting Parties, each for a one-year term, to rotate continuously among the Contracting Parties in alphabetical order.

   New Contracting Parties shall serve as chair in the order of their seniority as members, but only after all previous Contracting Parties have served.

   If a Contracting Party cannot serve as the Council of Ministers' chair for the year during which it should so serve, the Council appoints the Contracting Party that is, pursuant to the prior paragraphs, next in line for the chair.

   When the Contracting Party that was previously unable to serve as chair considers that it is able so to serve, it shall promptly so inform the Permanent Secretariat, requesting that the Council of Ministers take appropriate action.

Article 31: The Common Court of Justice and Arbitration is composed of nine judges.

Nevertheless, the Council of Ministers may, upon considering the size of the tasks and the availability of finances, fix the number of justices higher than as stipulated in the immediately preceding paragraph.

Judges of the Common Court of Justice and Arbitration are elected for a non-renewable term of seven years, from among the nationals of the Contracting Parties. They are chosen from among:

1. judges and magistrates having at least fifteen years of professional experience, and satisfying their respective countries' criteria for service in very senior judicial positions;
2. lawyers, being members of the Bar of a Contracting Party, and having at least fifteen years of professional experience;
3. law professors having at least fifteen years of professional experience.

One third of the members of the court must belong to the categories described at numbers 2 and 3 of the prior paragraph.

The Court may not include more than one national of any Contracting Party.

This article shall be applied in accordance with regulations promulgated pursuant to article 19, above.

Article 39: After soliciting the opinion of the Common Court of Justice and Arbitration, its Preside shall appoint a Chief Clerk of the Court from among chief clerks having performed such functions for at least fifteen years and having been nominated by the Contracting Parties.

After soliciting the opinion of the Court, the President shall also appoint the Secretary General charged with the responsibility to assist the Court in the discharging its obligation to administer arbitration proceedings, in accordance with the criteria defined in regulations promulgated by the Council of Ministers.

Upon the request of the Chief Clerk or of the General Secretary, as appropriate, the President shall delegate other duties.

Article 40: The Permanent Secretariat is the executive of OHADA. It is managed and directed by a Permanent Secretary appointed by the Council of Ministers for a four-year term, renewable once.

The Permanent Secretary represents OHADA and shall assist the Council of Ministers.

The appointment and powers of the Permanent Secretary, and the organization and operation of the Permanent Secretariat, are defined by regulations promulgated by the Council of Ministers.

Article 41: A centre of training and continuing education, and of study and analysis of business law, is hereby created, to be known as the Regional Training Center for Legal Officers (E.R.S.U.M.A.).

The center is attached to the Permanent Secretariat.

The name and purpose of the center may be modified by regulations promulgated by the Council of Ministers.

The center's executive is a Director General appointed by the Council of Ministers for a four-year term, renewable once.

The center's structure, operation, resources and obligations are defined by regulations of the Council of Ministers.

Article 42: OHADA's working languages are: French, English, Spanish and Portuguese.

Until such time as they have been translated into the other languages, all documents already published in French shall continue to have full effect. In the event of differences among the texts in the various languages, the French version will control.

Article 43: OHADA's resources are as follows:

(*a*) Contracting Parties' annual contributions, in accordance with terms stipulated in regulations promulgated by the Council of Ministers;
(*b*) assistance provided in accordance with agreements entered into between OHADA and Contracting Parties or international organizations;
(*c*) gifts and bequests.

The annual contributions of the Contracting Parties shall be determined by the Council of Ministers.

The Council of Ministers shall have the sole authority to approve agreements contemplated by paragraph (b), above, and gifts and bequests contemplated by paragraph (c), above.

Article 45: OHADA's annual budget shall be adopted by the Council of Ministers.

The annual financial statements for each accounting period shall be certified by commissaries of accounts appointed by the council of Ministers, and shall be presented to the Council of Ministers for approval.

Article 49 In accordance with regulations, the civil servants and employees of OHADA, the judges of the Common Court of Justice and Arbitration, and the arbitrators appointed or confirmed by said Court, shall all benefit from diplomatic privileges and immunities in the performance of their duties.

As appropriate, the Council of Ministers may remove such immunities and privileges.

Further, the judges may be sued for acts outside the performance of their official duties only upon authorization of the Court.

Article 57: Instruments of ratification and instruments of accession shall be deposited with the Government of Senegal, which shall be the Depositary Government. It shall deliver a copy of each such instrument to the Permanent Secretariat.

Article 59: The Depositary Government shall register the Treaty with the African Union, and with the United Nations in accordance with article 102 of the Charter of the United Nations.

The Depositary Government shall deliver to the Permanent Secretariat a copy of the Treaty, so registered.

Article 61: The Treaty may be amended or revised if a written request to this effect is sent by a Contracting Party to OHADA's Permanent Secretariat, which then forwards it to the Council of Ministers.

The Council of Ministers shall study the subject and purpose of the request, and the scope of the proposed modification.

The amendment or revision must be adopted in the same manner as was the Treaty, upon the request of the Council of Ministers.

Article 63: This Treaty, prepared in duplicate in French, English, Spanish and Portuguese, shall be deposited in the archives of the Government of the Republic of Senegal, which will submit a certified conformed copy to each of the Contracting Parties.

ARTICLE 2

This Treaty shall become effective sixty (60) days after the date of deposit of the eighth instrument of ratification.

The instruments of ratification and the instruments of accession shall be deposited with the Government of Senegal, which shall be the Depositary Government. It shall deliver a copy of each such instrument to the Permanent Secretary.

The Depositary Government shall register this Treaty with the African Union, and with the United Nations in accordance with article 102 of the Charter of the United Nations.

The Depositary Government shall deliver to the Permanent Secretariat a copy of this Treaty, so registered.

The Council of Ministers shall approve the consolidated text of the revised Treaty.

In witness whereof, the undersigned Heads of State and of Government and plenipotentiaries have set their hands and seals below, on this Treaty.

Made at Quebec, this 17th day of October, 2008

The President of the Republic of Benin,
Boni YAYI

The President of Burkina Faso,
Blaise COMPAORE

The President of the Republic of Cameroon,
Paul BIYA

The President of the Central African Republic,
François BOZIZE

The President of the Union of the Comoros,
Hamed Abdallah SAMBI

The President of the Republic of Congo,
Denis SASSOU N'GUESSO

For the President of the Republic of Côte d'Ivoire,
Youssouf BAKAYOKO,
Minister of Foreign Affairs

The President of the Republic of Gabon,
El Hadj OMAR BONGO ONDIMBA

For the President of the Republic of Guinea,
Ahmed SOUARE,
Prime Minister

For the President of the Republic of Guinea-Bissau,
Maria da Conceição NOBRE CABRAL,
Minister of Foreign Affairs

The President of the Republic of Equatorial Guinea,
Teodoro OBIANG NGUEMA MBASOGO

The President of the Republic of Mali,
Amadou Toumani TOURE

For the President of the Republic of Niger,
Seyni OUMAROU,
Prime Minister

The President of the Republic of Senegal,
Abdoulaye WADE

The President of the Republic of Chad,
Idriss DEBY ITNO

For the President of the Republic of Togo,
Gilbert FOSSOUN HOUNGBO,
Prime Minister

Appendix 4

OHADA: Selections from the Uniform Acts

All the sections referred to in the text, exclusive of footnotes, are set out below and are taken from the unofficial translations available at www.ohada.com and www.juriscope.org.

1. Uniform Act Relating to Commercial Companies and Economic Interest Groups

Articles 1-36

Article 1: Every commercial company, including those in which the State or a corporate body governed by public law is a partner, whose registered office is located on the territory of one of the Contracting States to the Treaty on the Harmonization in Africa of Business Law (hereinafter referred to as "Contracting States") shall be subject to the provisions of this Uniform Act.

All economic interest groups shall equally be subject to the provisions of this Uniform Act.

Besides, commercial companies and economic interest groups shall be subject to the laws which are not contrary to the provisions of this Uniform Act applicable in the Contracting States of their registered office.

Article 2: The provisions of this Uniform Act are mandatory, except in cases where the Act explicitly authorizes a sole partner or the partners of a company to substitute contractual provisions between them for those of this Uniform act or to supplement the provisions of this Uniform Act with their own provisions.

Article 3: Any persons, whatever their nationality, wishing to engage in a commercial activity in the form of a company on the territory of one of the Contracting States, shall choose a form of company which suits the activity envisaged from among those provided for by this Uniform Act.

The persons referred to in the preceding paragraph may also elect, under the conditions provided for by this Uniform Act, to form an economic interest group.

Article 4: A commercial company shall be formed by two or more persons who agree, by contract, to assign assets in cash or in kind to an activity for the purpose of sharing profits or benefiting from savings that may derive therefrom. The partners of the company shall accept to bear losses under the conditions stipulated in this Uniform Act.

A commercial company shall be formed in the common interest of the partners.

Article 5: A commercial company may also be created, as provided by this Uniform Act, by a single person, referred to a "sole proprietor", on the basis of a written document.

Article 6: The commercial nature of a company shall be determined by its form or object. Private Companies, Sleeping Partnerships, private limited companies and public limited companies are commercial companies by virtue of their form, irrespective of their object.

Article 7: Any natural person or corporate body may be a partner in a commercial company where he is not subject to any prohibition, incapacity or incompatibility as defined notably in the Uniform Act Relating to General Commercial Law.

Article 8: Minors and legally incapacitated persons may not be partners in a company where their liability for the company's debts exceeds their contributions.

Article 9: A husband and wife may not be partners in a company in which they shall be indefinitely or jointly and severally liable for the company's debts.

Article 10: The Articles of Association shall be established by a notarial deed or by any other instrument that ensures legal validity in the State of the company's registered office. Such instrument, together with a certification of the writing and signatures of all the parties, shall be deposited as originals in a notary's office. They may be amended only by the same procedure.

Article 11: Where the Articles of Association are drawn up in a private document, as many original copies shall be established as shall be needed to deposit one copy in the company's registered office and to fulfill all the required formalities. A copy of the Articles of Association on plain unheaded paper shall be given to each partner. However, in the case of Private Companies and Sleeping partnerships, one original copy shall be given to each partner.

Article 12: The Articles of Association shall either be a partnership deed, in the case where there are several partners, or a unilateral deed of intent, in the case of a sole proprietor.

Article 13: The Articles of Association shall contain the following information:

1. the form of the company;
2. the name of the company, followed by its acronym where necessary;
3. the nature and field of the company's activity which constitute its object;
4. the company's registered office;
5. its duration;

6. the identity of contributors in cash and, for each of them, the amount of their contribution and the number and value of the shares handed over in exchange for each contribution;
7. the identity of contributors in kind, the nature and value of the contribution made by each of them, the number and value of the shares handed over in exchange for each contribution;
8. the identity of persons enjoying special benefits and the nature of such benefits;
9. the amount of the registered capital;
10. the number and value of shares issued, stating, where necessary, the various classes of shares;
11. the provisions relating to the distribution of profits, the constitution of reserves and the distribution of the bonus after liquidation;
12. the rules governing its operation.

Article 14: Every company shall have a name which shall be mentioned in its Articles of Association.

Article 15: Unless otherwise provided for in this Uniform Act, the name of one or more partners or former partners may be included in the company name.

Article 16: A company may not take the name of another company which is already registered in the Trade and Personal Property Credit Register.

Article 17: The company name shall appear on all deeds and documents from the company to third parties, especially letters, bills, notices and various publications. It shall be preceded or followed immediately by an indication of the form of the company, the amount of its registered capital, the address of its registered office and its registration number in the Trade and Personal Property Credit Register.

Article 18: The company name may be changed under the conditions stipulated in this Uniform Act for amending the Articles of Association for each form of company.

Article 19: Every company shall have an object which shall constitute the company's activity and which shall be identified and described in the Articles of Association.

Article 20: Every company shall have a lawful object.

Article 21: Where the company is engaged in a regulated activity, it shall comply with the special regulations governing such activity.

Article 22: The company's object may be changed under the conditions stipulated in this Uniform Act for amending the Articles of Association for each company.

Article 23: Every company shall have a registered office which shall be indicated in the Articles of Association.

Article 24: Partners shall decide on the location of the registered office either at the company's principal place of activity, or at the place where its administrative and financial services are concentrated.

Article 25: The registered office may not consist solely in a postal address. It shall be localized by an address and or a specific and adequate geographic indication.

Article 26: Third parties may rely on the statutory registered office but it may not be relied upon by the company as against them where the real registered office is located elsewhere.

Article 27: The registered office may be changed under the conditions stipulated in this Uniform Act for amending the Articles of Association for each form of company. However, it may be transferred to a different location in the same town by a simple decision of the company's management or administration.

Article 28: Every company shall be set up for a duration which shall be indicated in the Articles of Association.

The duration of the company may not exceed ninety-nine years.

Article 29: The existence of a company shall begin on the date on which it is entered in the Trade and Personal Property Credit Register, unless otherwise provided by this Uniform Act.

Article 30: The expiry of the term shall entail the automatic dissolution of the company, unless an extension has been decided upon the conditions laid down in Articles 32 et seq. of this Uniform Act.

Article 31: The duration of the company may be changed under the conditions laid down in this Uniform Act for the amendment of the Articles of Association for each form of company.

Article 32: The existence of a company may be extended one or more times.

Article 33: The extension of the duration of the company shall be done under the conditions laid down in this Uniform Act for the amendment of the Articles of Association for each form of company.

Article 34: The extension of the duration of a company shall not entail the creation of a new legal entity.

Article 35: The partners shall be consulted at least one year before the date of expiry of the company to decide whether or not to extend the duration of the company.

Article 36: Failing this, any partner may request the president of the competent court within whose jurisdiction the registered office is located to designate, by summary proceedings, a legal representative to initiate the consultation provided for in the preceding article.

Articles 97-98

Article 97: With the exception of Sleeping partnerships, all companies shall be registered in the Trade and Personal Property Credit Register.

Article 98: All companies shall have a legal personality with effect from the date of registration in the Trade and Personal Property Credit Register, unless otherwise provided for in this Uniform Act.

Articles 100-115

Article 100: A company shall be deemed to be under formation where it has not yet been incorporated.

Article 101: A company shall be deemed to be formed from the date of signature of its Articles of Association.

Prior to its registration, the existence of the company shall not be demurrable to third parties. However, third parties may avail themselves of the existence of the company.

Article 102: All persons who actively participate in transactions leading to the formation of a company shall be deemed to be founders thereof.

Their role shall begin with the first transactions or with the performance of the initial acts for the purpose of setting up the company. It shall end on the date on which the Articles of Association are signed by all the partners or the sole proprietor.

Article 103: The founders of a company shall be domiciled on the territory of one of the Contracting States.

Such domicile shall not consist solely in the possession of a postal address. It shall comprise an address or specific and adequate geographic indications.

Article 104: From the date of signature of the Articles of Association, company executives shall take over from the founders. Company executives shall act on behalf of the company already formed but not yet entered in the Trade and Personal Property Credit Register.

The powers and obligations of company executives shall be defined in accordance with the provisions of this Uniform Act and, where necessary, by the Articles of Association.

Article 105: Between the date on which a company is formed and that on which it is entered in the Trade and Personal Property Credit Register, relations among the partners shall be governed by the Partnership deed and by general rules of law in matters of contracts and obligations.

Article 106: Acts done and commitments entered into by the founders on behalf of a company under formation, before it is incorporated, shall be brought to the attention of the partners before signature of the Articles of Association where the company does not make a public call for capital during the initial meeting of shareholders, where the contrary applies.

Such acts and commitments shall be detailed in a statement referred to as "Statement of acts done and commitments made on behalf of the company under formation", with indications, for each of them, of the nature and extent of the company's liabilities should it decide to take them over.

Article 107: In the case of companies formed without a constituent meeting, the statement of acts and commitments referred to in Article 106 above shall be appended to the Articles of Association. Where the partners sign the Articles of Association and the statement, the company shall be deemed to have taken over the contracts and commitments described in the statement with effect from the date the company is entered in the Trade and Personal Property Credit Register.

Article 108: Acts done and commitments entered into on behalf of the company during its formation may also be taken over by the company after its incorporation provided they are approved at an ordinary meeting of shareholders, under the conditions laid down by this Uniform Act for each form of company, unless otherwise provided for by the Articles of Association. The meeting shall be fully informed of the nature and scope of each of the acts and commitments being proposed for take-over by the company. The persons who signed such acts and commitments shall not vote and their votes shall not be taken into account in determining the quorum and the majority.

Article 109: In the case of a company formed by a constituent meeting, the take-over of pre-incorporation acts and commitments shall be the subject of a special resolution taken during the constituent meeting, under the conditions laid down by this Uniform Act.

Article 110: Acts and commitments taken over by a duly constituted and registered company shall be deemed to have been made by the company from the origin.

Acts and commitments not taken over by the company under the conditions laid down by this Uniform Act shall not be binding on the company and the persons who made them shall have unlimited liability for the obligations they entail.

Article 111: The partners may, in the Articles of Association or in a separate deed, grant powers to one or more company executives, depending on the case, to enter into commitments on behalf of the company which, though fully formed, has not yet been entered in the Trade and Personal Property Credit Register, provided that such commitments are defined and their scope specified in the terms of reference. The subsequent registration of the company in the Trade and Personal Property Credit Register shall entail the taking over of such commitments.

Article 112: Any acts done beyond the scope of their terms of reference or are unrelated to such terms may be taken over by the company provided they have been approved by an ordinary meeting of shareholders under the conditions laid down by this Uniform Act for each type of company, unless otherwise provided by the Articles of Association. The partners involved in such acts shall not be entitled to vote and their votes shall not be taken into account for determining the quorum and the majority.

Article 113: The provisions of Article 110 of this Uniform Act shall apply.

Article 114: Notwithstanding the preceding provisions, the partners may agree not to register the company which shall then be referred to as "Sleeping partnership". It shall not have a legal personality.

Sleeping partnership shall be governed by the provisions of Articles 854 et seq. of this Uniform Act.

Article 115: Where, contrary to the provisions of this Uniform Act, the Articles of Association or, where necessary, the unilateral deed of intent is not established in writing and, consequently, that the company cannot be registered, the company shall be referred to as a "de facto company". It shall not have a legal personality.

A de facto company shall be governed by the provisions of Articles 864 et seq. of this Uniform Act.

Articles 270-277 (Private Unlimited Company)

Article 270: A private company shall be a company in which all the partners are traders and have unlimited liability, for the company's debts.

Article 271: The company's creditors may bring an action against a partner for the payment of private company's debts only 60 days at least after unsuccessfully notifying the company of such claim through an extra-judicial act.

This time limit may be extended by order of the president of the competent through summary proceedings without such extension exceeding 30 days.

Article 272: The partnership shall be known by a company name which shall be immediately preceded or followed by the word «Private company» or by the abbreviation «P.C.», written in legible characters.

Article 273: The registered capital shall be broken down into shares of the same face value.

Article 274: The private company shares may be transferred only with the unanimous consent of the partners.

All provisions to the contrary shall be deemed to be unwritten.

Where the partners fail to reach unanimity, the transfer shall not take place, but the company's Articles of Association may make provision for a redemption procedure to enable the transferring partner to withdraw.

Article 275: The transfer of shares shall be evidenced in writing.

It may be relied upon as against the company only after the fulfillment of one of the following formalities:

1. notification to the company of the transfer by means of a bailiff's writ;
2. acceptance of the transfer by the company in a notarial deed;
3. deposit of the original of the transfer deed at the registered office against issuance by the manager of an attestation of deposit.

It shall not be binding on a third party except after compliance with the above formalities and after publication by way of an annexed deposit in the Trade and Personal Property Credit Register.

Article 276: The Articles of Association shall organize the management of the company.

They may appoint one or more managers who may be partners or not, natural persons or corporate bodies, or provide for such appointment in a subsequent instrument.

Where the manager is a corporate body, its officials shall be subject to the same conditions and obligations and shall incur the same civil and criminal liability as if they were managers on their own account, notwithstanding the joint and several liability of the corporate body they are managing.

Where the management is not organized by the Articles of Association, all the partners shall be deemed to be managers.

Article 277: Where the manager's powers are not defined by the Articles of Associations, the manager may, in his relations with partners, perform all acts of management in the company's interest. In the event of several managers, each shall have the same powers as if he were the sole manager of the company, save the right to object to any transaction before it is concluded.

In his relations with third parties, the manager shall commit the company by acts falling within the company's objects.

In the event of several managers, each of them shall have the same powers as if he were the sole manager of the company.

Any objection made by a manager to the action of another manager shall have no effect with respect to third parties, unless it is established that they were aware of such objection.

The provisions of the Articles of Association limiting the powers of managers resulting from this article shall not be demurrable to third parties.

Articles 293-300 (Sleeping, or Limited Partnership)

Article 293: A sleeping partnership is a partnership in which one or more partners are indefinitely, jointly and severally liable for the company's debts, referred to as «active partners», coexist with one or more partners liable for the company's debts up to the limit of their shares, referred to as « sleeping partners » and whose capital is broken down into partnership shares.

Article 294: A sleeping partnership shall be referred to by a name which shall be immediately preceded or followed by the words « sleeping partnership » or by the abbreviation « S.P. ».

The name of a sleeping partner shall under no circumstances be included in the partnership name, otherwise the latter shall be liable for the debts of the partnership without limit.

Article 295: The Articles of Association of the sleeping partnership shall include the following information:

1. the amount or value of all the partners' contributions;
2. the fraction of this amount or value belonging to each active or sleeping partner;
3. the overall share of the active partners and the share of each sleeping partner in the profit-sharing or in the bonus after liquidation.

Article 296: Partnership shares may be transferred only with the consent of all the partners.
However, the Articles of Association may stipulate:

1. that the shares held by the sleeping partners shall be freely transferable between partners ;
2. that the shares held by sleeping partners may be transferred to third parties outside the sleeping partnership with the consent of all the active partners and by a majority in number and capital of the sleeping partners ;
3. that an active partner may transfer part of his shares to a sleeping partner or to a third party outside the partnership with the consent of all the active partners and the majority in number and capital of the sleeping partners.

Article 297: The transfer of shares shall be recorded in a written document.

It may be binding on the company only after the following formalities have been fulfilled:

1. notification to the company of the transfer by means of a bailiff's writ;
2. acceptance of the transfer by the company in a notarial deed;
3. deposit of the original transfer deed at the registered office against an attestation of deposit issued by the manager.

The transfer of shares may be demurrable to third parties only after the fulfillment of the above formalities and after publication by entry in the Trade and Personal Property Credit Register.

Article 298: A sleeping partnership shall be managed by all the active partners unless otherwise provided by the Articles of Association which may appoint one or more managers from among the active partners, or provide for the appointment of such manager(s) by a subsequent instrument, under the same conditions and with the same powers as in a partnership.

Article 299: A sleeping partner(s) may not perform any act of external management, even by virtue of a power of attorney.

Article 300: In the event of violation of the prohibition mentioned in the preceding article, the sleeping partner(s) shall, be indefinitely, jointly and severally liable with the active partners for the company's debts and commitments resulting from any administrative acts performed by them.

Depending on the number and gravity of these acts, they may be liable for all commitments of the company or only for a few.

Articles 309-316 (Private Limited [Liability] Company)

Article 309: A private limited company shall be a company in which the partners are liable for the company's debts up to the limit of their contributions and their rights are represented by company shares.

It may be formed by a natural person or a corporate body, or by two or more natural persons or corporate bodies.

Article 310: It shall be referred to by a company name which must be immediately preceded or followed by the words "private limited company" or the abbreviation "Ltd" written in legible characters.

Article 311: The registered capital of a private limited liability company shall be at least one million (1000 000) CFA francs. It shall be divided into equal shares whose face value may not be less than five thousand (5 000) CFA francs.

Article 312: The Articles of Association shall contain the evaluation of each contribution in kind and a stipulation of special benefits.

The evaluation shall be carried out by a shares auditor where the value of the contribution or the benefits in question, or the value of the overall contributions or benefits in question is more than five million (5, 000,000) CFA francs.

The shares auditor who shall be chosen from a list of auditors following the procedure laid down in Article 694 et seq. of this Uniform Act, shall be unanimously designated by the future partners or, failing this, by the president of the competent court, at the request of all or one of the company's founders.

The shares auditor shall draw up a report to be appended to the Articles of Association.

In the absence of an evaluation made by a shares auditor or where such evaluation is disregarded, the partners shall, indefinitely, jointly and severally liable for the evaluation made of the contributions in kind and the special benefits stipulated for a period of five years.

The obligation to provide guarantees shall concern only the value of contributions at the time the capital is being constituted or increased and not the maintenance of the said value.

Article 313: Funds derived from the payment for shares shall be immediately deposited by the founder, against a receipt, in a bank account opened in the name of the company being formed or in a notary's office.

Article 314: The payment and deposit of funds shall be recorded by a notary within the jurisdiction of the court of the registered office by means of a notarial statement of subscription and payment indicating the list of subscribers with their full name and domicile, for natural persons, and company name, legal status and registered office, for corporate bodies, as well as the banks where those concerned are domiciled, where necessary, and the amounts paid by each of them.

The funds thus deposited shall be unavailable until the day of registration of the company in the Trade and Personal Property Credit Register. With effect from that day, they shall be put at the disposal of the managers duly appointed by the Articles of Association or by a subsequent instrument.

In the event where the company is not registered in the Trade and Personal Property Credit Register within a period of six months from the initial deposit of the funds at the bank or at a notary's office, the investors may either individually or collectively through an agent, request the president of the competent court to authorize withdrawal of the amount of their contributions.

Article 315: The partner(s) shall, under penalty of annulment of the company, participate in the Memorandum of Association in person or through their authorized agent with special powers.

Article 316: The initial managers and the partners responsible for the nullity of the company shall be jointly and severally liable towards the other partners and third parties for the damage resulting from the nullity.

Liability action shall be barred at the end of three years with effect from the date when the annulment decision became final.

Articles 385-389, 414-417, 435, 450, 462-465, 494 (Public Limited [Liability] Company)

Article 385: A public limited company shall be a company in which the liability of each shareholder for the debts of the company is limited to the amount of shares he has taken and his rights are represented by shares.

A public limited company may have only a single shareholder.

Article 386: A public limited company shall be known by a company name which shall immediately be preceded or followed in legible characters by the words: "public limited company" or the abbreviations: "plc" and the method of administration of the company as provided for in Article 414 below.

Article 387: The minimum authorized capital shall be fixed at ten million (10, 000,000) CFA francs. It shall be divided into shares of a face value of not less than ten thousand (10,000) CFA francs.

Article 388: The capital of a public limited company shall be fully subscribed before the date of signature of its Articles of Association or holding of the constituent general meeting.

Article 389: At least one quarter of the face value of shares representing contributions in cash shall be paid up during capital subscription.

The rest shall be paid up within a period of not more than three years from the date of registration of the company in the Trade and Personal Property Credit Register, in accordance with the terms and conditions laid down by the Articles of Association or by a decision of the board of directors or the managing director.

Article 414: The method of administration of each public limited company shall be clearly defined by its Articles of Association which shall choose between:

- a public limited company with a board of directors; or
- a public limited company with a managing director.

A public limited company may, during its life, change at any time its method of administration and management.

The decision shall be taken by an extraordinary general meeting of shareholders which shall amend the Articles of Association accordingly.

The amendments shall be entered in the Trade and Personal Property Credit Register.

Article 415: A public limited company with a board of directors shall be managed either by a chairman and managing director or by a chairman of the board of directors and a general manager.

Article 416: A public limited company may be administered by a board of directors comprising not less than three and not more than twelve members.

Article 417: Not more than one-third of the members of the board shall be non shareholders of the company.

Directors who are not shareholders of the company shall be subject to the provisions of Articles 416 to 434 of this Uniform Act.

Article 435: The board of directors shall have the widest powers to act in all circumstances on behalf of the company.

It shall exercise its powers within the limits of the objects of the company and subject to those expressly conferred by this Uniform Act to meetings of shareholders.

The board of directors shall, in particular:

1. define the company's objectives and guidelines for its administration;
2. control, on a permanent basis, the management of the chairman and managing director or of the general manager, depending on the method of management adopted;
3. adopt the accounts of each fiscal year.

The provisions of the Articles of Association or the decisions of the general meeting restricting the powers of the board of directors shall not be demurrable to third parties.

Article 450: Directors, general managers and assistant general managers, as well as their spouse, ascendants or descendants and through other third parties shall, under penalty of the agreement being declared null and void, be forbidden to contract, in any form whatsoever, loans from the company, to have it grant them a current account overdraft or otherwise, and to have the company provide security or guarantee for their commitments towards third parties.

This prohibition shall not apply to corporate bodies that are members of the board of directors. However, their permanent representative, when acting in his personal interest shall also be subject to the provisions of the first paragraph of this article.

Where the company runs a banking or financial institution, such prohibition shall not apply to ordinary transactions concluded under normal terms.

Article 462: The board of directors shall appoint a chairman and managing director from among its members.

Under penalty of his appointment being declared null, the chairman and managing director shall be a natural person.

Article 463: The term of office of the chairman and managing director shall not exceed his term of office as director.

The chairman and managing director's mandate shall be renewable.

Article 464: No person shall hold simultaneously more than three offices as chairman and managing director of public limited companies having their registered office on the territory of the same Contracting State.

Likewise, a term of office as chairman and managing director shall not be held concurrently with more than two appointments as managing director or general manager of public limited companies having their registered office on the territory of the same Contracting State.

The provisions of paragraphs 2 and 3 of Article 425 of this Uniform Act relating to the plurality of offices as director shall be applicable to the chairman and managing director.

Article 465: The chairman and managing director shall preside over the meetings of the board of directors and the general meetings of shareholders.

He shall ensure the general management of the company and represent same in its relations with third parties.

He shall, for the performance of his duties, be given the widest possible powers which he shall exercise within the limits of the objects of the company and subject to the powers expressly conferred on the general meetings or specially reserved for the board of directors by the laws and regulations in force.

The company shall, in its relations with third parties, be bound even by the acts of the chairman and managing director which do not fall within the scope of the objects of the company, under the conditions and within the limits laid down in Article 122 of this Uniform Act.

The provisions of the Articles of Association, the decisions of general meetings or of the board of directors restricting the powers of the chairman and managing director shall not be demurrable to third parties acting in good faith.

Article 494: Public limited liability companies with not more than three shareholders may not form a board of directors and may appoint a managing director who shall be responsible for administering and managing the company. In this case, the provisions of the first paragraph of Article 417 shall not apply.

Articles 869-879 (Economic Interest Group)

Article 869: An economic interest group shall be one which has the exclusive object of putting in place for a specified duration all the means necessary to facilitate or develop the economic activity of its members and to improve or increase income from the said activity.

Its activity shall mainly be connected with the economic activity of its members and shall not be of an auxiliary nature in relation thereto.

Article 870: The economic interest group shall not by itself give rise to the realization or sharing of profits. It may be formed without capital.

Article 871: Two or more natural persons or corporate bodies, including persons exercising a liberal profession governed by a legislative or statutory instrument or whose title is protected, may form between them an economic interest group.

The rights of members of the group may not be represented by negotiable instruments. Any clause to the contrary shall be deemed to be unwritten.

Article 872: An economic interest group shall have corporate personality and full capacity with effect from registration in the Trade and Personal Property Credit Register.

Article 873: The members of the economic interest group shall be liable for the debts of the group on their assets proper. However, a new member may, where the contract permits, be exempted from the debts contracted before he joined the group. The exoneration decision shall be published.

The members of the economic interest group shall be jointly and severally liable for payment of the debts of the group, unless otherwise agreed with a contracting third party.

Article 874: The creditors of the group may take action for the settlement of debts against a partner only after unsuccessfully notifying the group by an extra-judicial act.

Article 875: An economic interest group may issue bonds under the general conditions of issue of such bonds where the group exclusively comprises companies authorized to issue bonds.

Article 876: Subject to the provisions of this Uniform Act, a contract shall determine the organization of the economic interest group and shall freely lay down the contribution of each member to the debts of the group. Failing this, each member shall bear an equal part of the debt.

During its existence, the group may accept new members under the conditions laid down by contract.

Any member may withdraw from the group under the conditions laid down in the contract, subject to having fulfilled his obligations.

The contract shall be in writing and shall be subject to the same conditions of publicity as the companies concerned by this Uniform Act.

It shall in particular contain the following details :

1. the name of the economic interest group ;
2. the name, trade name or corporate name, legal form, address of the domicile or head office and, as the case may be, the registration number in the Trade and Personal Property Credit Register of each member of the economic interest group ;
3. the duration for which the economic interest group is formed ;
4. the object of the economic interest group ;
5. the address of the registered office of the economic interest group.

Any amendments to the contract shall be drawn up and published under the same conditions as the contract itself. They shall be demurrable to third parties from the date of such publicity.

The deeds and documents emanating from the economic interest group intended for third parties, in particular letters, invoices, various notices and publications shall clearly show the name of the group, followed by the words « economic interest group » or the acronym "E.I.G."

Any violation of the provisions of the above paragraph shall be punished with penalty for simple offences.

Article 877: The general meeting of members of the economic interest group shall be competent to take any decision, including premature winding up or extension of the existence of the group under the conditions laid down in the contract.

The contract may provide that all or some decisions shall be taken under the conditions of quorum and majority it shall determine. Where the contract is silent, decisions shall be taken unanimously.

The contract may also allocate to each member of the economic interest group a number of votes different from that allocated to others. Failing this, each member shall have one vote.

Article 878: The meeting shall meet as of right at the request of at least one quarter of the members of the economic interest group.

Article 879: The economic interest group shall be administered by one or more natural persons or corporate bodies, provided that in the case of a corporate body, such corporate body shall designate a permanent representative, who shall incur the same civil and criminal liabilities as if he were a director in his own name.

Subject to this reserve, the contract or, failing that, the general meeting of members of the economic interest group shall freely organize the administration of the group and appoint the directors whose duties, powers and conditions of dismissal it shall determine.

In relations with third parties, a director shall commit the economic interest group for any act connected with the object of the group. No limitation of powers may be invoked against third parties.

2. Uniform Act on General Commercial Law

Articles 1-20, 25, 27, 38-39, 42 (commerçants: commercial operators, or traders)

Article 1: Every trader, be he a natural or legal person including all commercial companies of which a State or a person governed by public law is a member, as well as every economic interest group, whose place of business or registered office is situated on the territory of one of the Contracting States to the Treaty on the Harmonization of Business Law in Africa, (hereinafter referred to as "Contracting States"), shall be subject to the provisions of this Uniform Act.

Besides, every trader shall be subject to the laws which are not contrary to the provisions of this Uniform Act applicable in the Contracting State of his place of business or registered office.

Natural persons or corporate bodies, and economic interest groups, set up or being formed on the date of entry into force of this Uniform Act must harmonize the conditions under which they carry on their activity with this new legislation within a period of two years from the date of publication of this Uniform Act in the Official Gazette.

After this time limit, any party concerned may bring an action before the court of competent jurisdiction for such regularization to be ordered, where necessary under financial compulsion.

Article 2: Traders are persons whose regular occupation is to carry out commercial transactions.

Article 3: Commercial transactions shall include:

- the purchase of movable or immovable property for resale;
- banking, stock-exchange, currency exchange, brokerage and transit transactions;
- contracts between traders for business purposes;
- the industrial exploitation of mines, quarries and any natural resource deposit;
- rental of personal property;
- manufacturing, transportation and telecommunication operations;
- middlemen's business transactions such as commission, brokerage and agency, as well as middleman's operations relating to the purchase, underwriting, sale or rental of immovable property, businesses, shares in commercial companies or building societies; and
- transactions carried out by commercial companies.

Article 4: A bill of exchange, a promissory note, and a warrant shall, by virtue of their form, also be considered as commercial transactions.

Article 5: Proof of commercial transactions can be given by any means with respect to traders.

Article 6: No person shall engage in trading as a regular occupation unless he has the legal capacity to trade.

Article 7: A minor shall not have the status of trader or engage in trading unless he is emancipated.

The spouse of a trader shall not have the status of trader unless he or she carries out the transactions referred to under Articles 3 and 4 above as a regular occupation and separately from those of his or her spouse.

Article 8: No person shall engage in a commercial activity incompatible with his previous status.

There shall be no incompatibility unless it is provided for by a text.

The person invoking the incompatibility shall be bound to provide proof of it.

Transactions carried out by a person in a state of incompatibility shall nevertheless be valid with respect to third parties acting in good faith.

Third parties shall, where they so desire, take advantage of transactions carried out by a person who is in a situation of incompatibility, but the latter can take no advantage of such transactions.

Article 9: The exercise of a commercial activity shall be incompatible with the exercise of the following duties or occupations:

- civil servants and staff of public entities and State-owned Enterprises;
- Court officials and Auxiliary officers of Justice: Barrister, Bailiff, Auctioneer, Stock Exchange Broker, Notary, Court Registrar, Legal Administrator, and Liquidator;
- approved Chartered Accountant and approved Accounting Officer, Auditor, Consulting Lawyer, Ship-broker;
- more generally, any occupation the exercise of which is subject to regulations forbidding the exercise of such activity concurrently with a commercial occupation.

Article 10: No person shall carry on a commercial activity, directly or through an intermediary, where he is the subject of:

- a permanent or temporary general ban imposed by a court of one of the Contracting States, whether the said ban is imposed as a principal or accessory penalty;
- a ban imposed by a professional court; in this case, the ban shall apply only to the commercial activity concerned;
- a definite sentence of imprisonment for an ordinary law offence or a non suspended sentence of not less than three months imprisonment for a misdemeanour against property or an offence of an economic or financial nature.

Article 11: A temporary ban of more than 5 years as well as a permanent ban may be lifted, at the request of the convict, by the court that imposed the ban.

Such request shall be admissible only after the expiration of a period of 5 years from the day the ban was imposed.

A ban on the bankrupt shall end upon discharge, under the conditions and forms provided for in the Uniform Act regarding the collective procedures for the wiping up of payable accounts.

Article 12: Without prejudice to other sanctions, transactions carried out by a convict shall not be demurrable to third persons acting in good faith.

Good faith shall always be presumed.

However, such transaction shall be demurrable to the convict.

Article 13: Every corporate body or natural person who is a trader shall keep a day book in which his commercial transactions shall be recorded on a daily basis.

He shall equally keep a general ledger, with a general summary balance, as well as an inventory book.

These books shall be kept in accordance with the provisions of the Uniform Act relating to the organization and harmonization of business accounting.

Every corporate body which is a trader shall also comply with the provisions of the Uniform Act relating to the Law on commercial companies and economic interest groups and the Uniform Act relating to the organization and harmonization of business accounting.

Article 14: The day book and the inventory book shall mention the registration number of the natural person or corporate body concerned in the Trade and Personal Property Credit Register.

They shall be numbered and initialed by the President of the court of competent jurisdiction, or by the Judge delegated for this purpose.

They shall be kept without blank spaces or alterations of any kind.

Article 15: The trade books referred to under Article 13 above, which shall be regularly kept, may be admitted in evidence by the judge in disputes between traders.

Article 16: In the course of a dispute, the Judge may order, even as a matter of routine, the presentation of trade books, with a view to extracting information concerning the dispute.

Article 17: Every corporate body engaged in trading shall equally draw up, each year, a summary of its financial statements, in accordance with the provisions of the Uniform Act relating to the organization and harmonization of business accounting, and to the Uniform Act relating to commercial companies and economic interest groups.

Article 18: Obligations resulting from trade between traders, or between traders and non-trader, shall be barred after a period of five years where they are not subject to shorter limitation periods.

Article 19: The purpose of the Trade and Personal Property Credit Register shall be:

(1) for the registration of: a) natural persons having the status of trader, within the meaning of this Uniform Act; b) commercial companies and other corporate bodies subject to registration, as well as branches of foreign companies operating on the territory of the Contracting State.

The register shall also record entries and information on changes in the status and legal capacity of natural persons and corporate bodies that have occurred since their registration.

It shall also record documents the filing of which is provided for by the provisions of this Uniform Act and by those of the Uniform Act relating to the Law on commercial companies and economic interest groups.

(2) for entries relating to:

a) the pledging of shares;
b) the pledging of a business, and the preferential right of the seller of the business;
c) the pledging of professional equipment and motor vehicles;
d) the pledging of stocks;
e) the preferential rights of the Treasury, the Customs Administration and Social Security Institutions;
f) ownership reserve clauses;
g) leasing contracts.

Article 20: The Trade and Personal Property Credit Register shall be kept by the court Registry of competent jurisdiction, under the supervision of the President or a Judge delegated for this purpose.

Information entered in each Trade and Personal Property Credit Register shall be centralized in a National Card-Index.

Information entered in each National Card-Index shall be centralized in a Regional Card-Index kept at the Common Court of Justice and Arbitration.

Articles 25 & 27 (commerçants, continued)

Article 25: Every natural person having the status of trader as provided for in this Uniform Act shall, within the first month of operation of his business, apply to the Registry of the competent court within whose jurisdiction the business is operated for registration in the Trade and Personal Property Credit Register.

The application for registration shall indicate :

1. the full name and domicile of the applicant;
2. his date and place of birth;
3. his nationality;
4. where applicable, the name under which he runs the business and the sign used;
5. the activity or activities carried out, and the form of operation;
6. the date and place of marriage, the type of marriage property option adopted, clauses demurrable to third persons restricting the free disposal of property of the spouses or the absence of such clauses, actions for separation of property;
7. the full name, date and place of birth, domicile and nationality of persons with power to commit by their signature the responsibility of the applicant;
8. the address of the principal place of business and, where applicable, the address of each of the other subsidiaries or branches operated on the territory of the Contracting State;
9. where applicable, the nature and the place of operation of the activity of the last subsidiaries previously operated with an indication of their registration number (s) in the Trade and Personal Property Credit Register;
10. the date of commencement, by the applicant, of the operation of the principal business and, where applicable, the other subsidiaries.

Article 27: The companies and other corporate bodies referred to in the Uniform Act relating to the Law on commercial companies and economic interest groups shall apply for registration in the Trade and Personal Property Credit Register, within a month of their formation, to the Registry of the court within whose jurisdiction their registered office is located.

The application shall mention:

1. the business name;
2. where applicable, the commercial name, acronym or sign;
3. the activity or activities carried out;
4. the form of the company or corporate body;
5. the amount of the registered capital with indication of the amount of contributions in cash and an evaluation of contributions in kind;
6. the address of the registered office, and where applicable, that of the principal place of business and of each of the other subsidiaries;
7. the duration of the company or the corporate body as fixed by its articles of association;
8. the full name and domicile of business partners who have unlimited liability vis-à-vis the company's debts, with an indication of their date and place of birth, nationality, date and place of marriage, the type of marriage property option adopted and clauses demurrable to third persons restricting the free disposal of property of the spouses or the absence of such clauses, as well as actions for the separation of property;
9. the full name, date and place of birth, and domicile of managers, administrators or business partners with general power to commit the responsibility of the company or corporate body;
10. the full name, date and place of birth and domicile of Auditors where their designation is provided for by the Uniform Act relating to the Law on commercial companies and economic interest groups.

Articles 38, 39 &42 (commerçants, continued)

Article 38: Any person registered in the Trade and Personal Property Credit Register shall be presumed, save proof to the contrary, to have the status of trader within the meaning of this Uniform Act.

However, such presumption shall not be invoked with respect to economic interest groups.

Every natural person or corporate body registered in the Trade and Personal Property Credit Register shall be bound to indicate on its invoices, order forms, tariffs and commercial documents, as well as on every correspondence its number and place of registration in the Register.

Article 39: Natural persons and corporate bodies subject to registration in the Trade and Personal Property Credit Register who have not applied for registration within the prescribed deadline, shall not claim, until they are duly registered, the status of trader.

However, they shall not rely on their failure to have themselves registered in the Register in order to avoid the liabilities and obligations inherent in that status.

Article 42: Where the corporate body or natural person who is a trader fails to apply for registration within the prescribed time-limit, the competent court may, automatically or at the request of the Registry in charge of the Trade and Personal Property Credit Register, or any other applicant, take a decision ordering the party concerned to have his registration effected.

The competent court may, under the same conditions, order any natural person or corporate body registered in the Trade and Personal Property Credit Register to have either:

- information added to or amended in the Register;
- necessary information added or amendment made to the Register in case of an incorrect or incomplete declaration;
- its removal from the Register effected.

Articles 69-73 (commercial leases)

Article 69: The provisions of this Part shall be applicable, in towns of more than five thousand inhabitants, to all leases concerning immovable property falling under the following categories:

1. premises or buildings for commercial, industrial, handicraft or professional purposes;
2. secondary premises adjoining premises or a building for commercial, industrial, handicraft or professional purposes, provided that, where these secondary premises belong to different owners, the rental is intended for use

jointly and that such use is made known to the lessor at the time of conclusion of the lease;

3. non built-on estate on which buildings for industrial, commercial, handicraft or profession purposes have been constructed, either before or after conclusion of the lease, where such buildings are built or used with the consent or knowledge of the owner.

Article 70: The provisions of his Part shall also apply to industrial or commercial legal entities governed by public law and to public corporations whether they are lessors or lessees.

Article 71: A commercial lease shall be any agreement, even unwritten, between the owner of immovable property or part thereof falling within the scope of Article 69 of this Act and any natural person or corporate body allowing the latter to carry on any commercial, industrial, handicraft or professional activity on the premises with the consent of the owner.

Article 72: The parties shall freely determine the duration of leases.

A commercial lease may be concluded for a specified or unspecified duration.

Where the lease is unwritten or is of an unspecified duration, it shall be deemed to have been concluded for an unspecified duration.

Article 73: The lessor shall be bound to hand over the premises in good condition. He shall be presumed to have fulfilled this obligation:

- where the lease is verbal, or
- where the lessee has signed the lease without making any reserves concerning the state of the premises.

Articles 80-83 (commercial leases continued)

Article 80: The lessee shall pay the rent on the terms agreed upon to the lessor or his representative designated in the lease.

Article 81: The lessee shall be bound to use the premises leased with due diligence and in accordance with the specifications in the lease or, in the absence of any written agreement, according to the presumed use, depending on the circumstances.

Where the lessee puts the premises into use other than that of which they are intended, and as a result of which the lessor suffers damage, the latter could bring an action before the competent court to terminate the lease.

The same shall apply where the lessee carries on a connected or additional activity to that specified in the lease.

Article 82: The lessee shall be responsible for maintenance repairs.

He shall be answerable for deteriorations or losses due to lack of maintenance during the lease.

Article 83: The lessee who, for any reason other than the one provided for in Article 94 below, remains on the premises after the expiry of the lease against the wish of the lessor shall pay an occupancy allowance equal to the amount of the rent fixed during the duration of the lease, without prejudice to the eventual payment of damages.

Articles 103-105, 115-117 (fonds de commerce : business)

Article 103: A business shall comprise a series of resources that enable a trader to attract and maintain customers.

It shall comprise various tangible and intangible elements of property.

Article 104: A business shall obligatorily comprise customers and a sign or trade name.

These elements are referred to as goodwill.

Article 105: A business may also, provided that they are designated by name, comprise the following elements:

- fittings,
- fixtures,
- equipment,
- furniture,
- goods in stock,
- the right to a lease,
- operation licences,
- patents, trade marks, drawings and designs and any other intellectual property rights necessary for the operation of the business.

Article 115: The transfer of the business shall comply with the general rules of sale, subject to the provisions below, and the specific provisions governing the carrying on of certain commercial activities.

Article 116: The transfer of the business shall necessarily concern the goodwill as defined by Article 104 of this Uniform Act.

It may also concern the other elements of the business referred to in Article 105 above, provided that they are expressly stated in the transfer document.

The provisions of the preceding paragraphs shall not forbid the transfer of separate elements of the business.

Article 117: The sale of a business may be made either by a private document or by a notarial deed.

The provisions of this chapter shall apply to any document recording a transfer of a business, granted even subject to conditions, including the contribution of the business to a company.

Articles 137-139 (trade middlemen, trade intermediaries)

Article 137: A trade middleman is a person who has the capacity to act or who purports to act, on a regular basis and as an occupation, on behalf of another person, called the principal, for the purposes of concluding a commercial contract of sale with a third party.

Article 138: A trade middleman is a trader; he must comply with the conditions provided for in Articles 6 to 12 of this Uniform Act.

The conditions of access to professions of middleman may in addition be supplemented by conditions specific to each category of middlemen provided for in this Book.

A trade middleman may be an individual or a corporate body.

Article 139: The provisions of this Book shall govern not only the conclusion of contracts by the middleman, but also any transaction carried out by the latter in view of concluding or performing the said contract.

They shall apply to all relations between the principal, the middleman and the third party.

They shall apply, whether the middleman acts in his own name, in the case of a commission agent or a broker, or on behalf of the principal, in the case of a commercial agent.

Articles 202-205, 210, 219, 233, 245, 283, 285-286 (commercial sale)

Article 202: The provisions of this Book shall apply to contracts of sale of goods between traders, be they natural persons or corporate bodies.

Article 203: The provisions of this Book shall not govern:

1. sales to consumers, that is to say any person acting for purposes outside his occupational activity;
2. sales after seizure, sales by order of the court and sales by auction;
3. sales of chattels, negotiable instruments, currencies or foreign exchange and transfers of debts.

Article 204: The provisions of this Book shall not apply to contracts in which the major part of the obligation of the party that delivers the goods shall be the supply of manpower or other services.

Article 205: Apart from the provisions of this Book, the commercial sale shall be subject to Ordinary Law rules.

Article 210: A proposal to conclude a contract sent to one or more specific persons shall constitute an offer where it is sufficiently specific and indicates the intentions of the offeror to be bound in case of acceptance.

A proposal shall be sufficiently specific where it indicates the goods, and expressly or implicitly determines the quantity and price of the goods or provides guidelines which make such determination possible.

Article 219: The seller shall be bound, under the conditions provided for in the contract and in this Book, to deliver the goods and to hand over, where need be, documents related to them, to ascertain that they are in conformity with the order and to give a guarantee.

Article 233: The buyer shall be bound, under the conditions laid down in the contract and in accordance with the provisions of this Part, to pay the price and take delivery of the goods.

Article 245: A party may bring an action before the competent court for authorization to defer the fulfillment of his obligations where it appears, after conclusion of the contract, that the other party shall not fulfill an essential part of his obligations due to:

1. a serious lack of capacity to perform the contract, or
2. his insolvency, or
3. the manner in which he is preparing to perform or is performing the contract.

Article 283: Unless otherwise agreed upon between the parties, the transfer of ownership shall take place from the moment the buyer takes delivery of the goods sold.

Article 285: The transfer of ownership shall entail the transfer of risks.

However, the loss or deterioration of goods incurred after the transfer of risks to the buyer shall not relieve him of his obligation to pay the purchase price, except where such loss or deterioration is an act of the seller.

Article 286: Where the contract of sale involves the transportation of goods, the risks shall be transferred to the buyer as soon as the goods are handed over to the first carrier.

The fact that the seller is authorized to keep the documents representing the goods shall not affect the transfer of risks.

3. Uniform Act Organizing Secured Transactions and Guaranties

Articles 1-2, 4, 24, 28, 49, 122, 150

Article 1: Securities shall be the means offered a creditor by the law of each Contracting State or agreement between the parties to guarantee the execution of obligations, whatever their legal nature may be.

Securities in the domain of fluvial, maritime and airspace law shall be regulated by specific legislation.

Article 2: A collateral security shall consist in the undertaking by one person to be answerable for the obligation of the principal debtor in case of the latter's default or at the first call of the beneficiary of the guarantee.

A secured debt shall consist in the right of the creditor to ask for payment, preferentially, from the proceeds of the sale of personalty or realty used to guaranty the debtor's obligation.

Article 4: Whatever the nature of the obligation guaranteed, the surety-bond shall not be presumed. Under penalty of being declared void, it shall be expressly agreed upon between the guarantor and the creditor.

A surety-bond shall be recorded in a deed bearing the signature of the two parties and an indication in the guarantor's handwriting of the maximum amount guaranteed in words and in figures. Where the two differ, the surety-bond shall be good for the amount in words.

A guarantor who does not or is unable to write shall be assisted by two witnesses who shall vouch for his identity and presence in the bond instrument and, furthermore, attest to the fact that the nature and effects of the deed have been explained to him. The presence of attesting witnesses shall dispense the guarantor from fulfilling the formalities referred to in the preceding paragraph.

The provisions of this article shall also apply to surety-bonds required by the law of each Contracting State or by a court decision.

Article 24: The guarantor may take action for payment against the principal debtor or request that his rights be maintained in the latter's estate even before paying the creditor:

- as soon as proceedings are taken against him;
- where the debtor has defaulted or is unable to meet his liabilities;
- where the debtor did not discharge him within the agreed time limit;
- where the debt has fallen due to shortening of the period under which it was contracted.

Article 28: A letter of guaranty shall be an agreement by which, at the request or on the instructions of the principal, the guarantor undertakes to pay a fixed amount to the beneficiary, upon the latter's first call.

A counter-guaranty letter shall be an agreement by which, at the request or on the instructions of the principal or the guarantor, the counter-guarantor undertakes to pay a fixed amount to the guarantor, upon the latter's first call.

Article 49: Whatever be the nature of the debt guaranteed, the pledge contract may not be binding on third parties unless it is recorded in writing, is duly registered and contains a statement of the amount owed and the kind, nature and quantity of personal property pledged.

However, the written document shall not be necessary in the case where the national law of each Contracting State allows for freedom of proof depending on the amount of the recognizance.

Article 122: Any contractual or legal document to mortgage property shall be entered in the land register in accordance with the rules relating to the notification of landed property transactions.

Registration shall confer on the creditor a right whose scope shall be defined by the national law of each Contracting State and by the provisions set out in the land certificate.

A duly published mortgage shall be ranked on the day of registration, unless otherwise stipulated by the law, and shall maintain such rank until the publication of its extinction.

Where the real property rights which have been mortgaged consist in the breaking up of such real property rights as usufruct, land surface rights, long lease or building lease, the registration of the mortgage must also be notified, by extra-judicial act, to the owner, owner of the soil and subsoil or lessor.

Article 150: All previous provisions repugnant to those of this Uniform Act are hereby repealed. This Uniform Act shall apply only to securities granted or established after its entry into force.

Any security granted, established or created prior to this Uniform Act and in accordance with the laws then in force shall remain subject to that law until its extinction.

4. Uniform Act on Collective Procedures for the Clearing of Debts (Bankruptcy Law)

Articles 2, 7, 18, 174, 183

Article 2:

1. Preventive settlement shall be proceedings aimed at avoiding the cessation of payments or the cessation of activity by a company or at making it possible to wipe off its debts through a preventive composition agreement.

   Preventive settlement shall apply to any natural person or corporate body that is a trader and to any non-trading private corporate body, to any public corporation in the form of a private corporate body, which, no matter the nature of its debts, is facing a difficult but not irremediable economic and financial situation.

2. Legal redress shall be proceedings aimed at safeguarding a company and at wiping off its debts through composition with creditors.

3. Liquidation of property shall be proceedings aimed at selling the assets of a debtor in order to pay his debts.

4. Legal redress and liquidation of property shall apply to any natural person or corporate body that is a trader, to any non-trading private corporate body and to any public corporation in the form of a private corporate body that stops payments.

Article 7: The debtor shall, at the same time as the documents [for preventive settlement] provided for under Article 6 above or no later than thirty days following the deposit of the said documents, under penalty of his petition being declared inadmissible, lodge a proposal of a preventive composition agreement specifying the measures and conditions envisaged to redress the company, in particular:

- modalities for continuing the operation of the company such as request for deadlines and debt cancellations, partial transfer of assets specifying the property to be transferred; transfer or management under lease of a branch of activity forming a business; transfer or management under lease of the entire company, without such modalities being restrictive and exclusive of each other;
- persons who have to execute the composition agreement and all the commitments entered into by them and needed to redress the company; modalities for maintaining and financing the company, and settling debts contracted prior to the decision provided for under Article 8 below as well as, where necessary, the guarantees given to ensure the execution; such commitments and guarantees may consist, in particular, in subscribing to an increase of the registered capital of the company by former or new partners, the opening of credits by banking or financial establishments, the continuation of the execution of contracts concluded before the petition and the provision of securities;
- layoffs for economic reasons which shall be carried out under the conditions laid down by labour law provisions; and

- replacement of managers.

Article 18: The ratification of the preventive composition agreement shall render same binding on all the creditors prior to the preventive settlement decision whether their claims are unsecured or guaranteed by a security under the deadline and write-off conditions they granted the debtor, without prejudice to the provisions of Article 15 (2) above. The same shall apply to guarantors for the debts of the debtor contracted prior to the said decision.

Creditors with secured debts shall not lose their guarantees but shall enforce them only in the event of annulment or cancellation of the preventive composition agreement to which they consented or which has been imposed on them.

The debtor's guarantors and co-obligators shall not avail themselves of the deadlines and write-offs granted under the preventive composition agreement.

Time shall stop running as concerns creditors who, due to the preventive composition agreement, cannot claim their rights or institute actions.

The debtor shall recover his freedom to administer and dispose of his property as soon as the preventive settlement decision becomes final.

Article 174: The decision to close operations for inadequacy of assets shall enable each creditor to recover his right to institute individual actions.

To this end, the provisions of Article 171 above shall apply.

Article 183: Where legal redress or liquidation of property of a corporate body results in an inadequacy of assets, the competent court may, in the case where a management error contributed to such inadequacy of assets, decide, at the request of the receiver of even of its own motion that the corporate body's debts will be borne in whole or in part, with or without joint and several liability, by all or some of the managers.

The receiver's writ of summons shall be served on each manager implicated at least eight days before the court session. Where the competent court is examining the matter on its own motion, the President of the court shall have the court registrar summon them by extrajudicial act within the same period.

The competent court shall take a decision as soon as possible, after hearing the official receiver in his report and the managers in camera.

5. Uniform Act on Simplified Recovery Procedures and Measures of Execution

The English translation is taken only from www.juriscope.org. The Commentaries to this English translation were provided by Fonkwe Joseph Fongang, Puisne Judge, Supreme Court of Cameroon, and Lucy Asuagbor, Chief Justice, South West Court of Appeal, Buea, Cameroon, with the collaboration of François Anoukaha, Dean, Faculty of Law of Dschang (Cameroon).

Articles 30, 32, 49, 130

Article 30: Execution of a writ and preventative measures shall not apply to persons enjoying immunity from execution.

However, any unquestionable debts due for payment belonging to public corporations or enterprises, regardless of their form and mission, may equally be compensated with unquestionable debts due for payment belonging to any person owing them, subject to reciprocity.

The debts of the corporations and enterprises referred to in the preceding paragraph may only be considered as unquestionable, within the meaning of this article, where they arise from an acknowledgement by the said corporations and enterprises of the debts or a writ enforceable on the territory of the State where the corporations and enterprises are based.

Comment:

This article states as a principle that execution does not levy against persons who benefit from immunity from execution. Although such persons have not been enumerated it may be conjectured by reference to paragraph 2 that such persons include the state and its entities as Councils and Universities.

This provision consecrates the general principle whereby execution does not levy against the State and its entities. The rationale is that the States is considered as being always solvent neither does it die. However, this does not mean that the State does not pay its debts. Any debts owed by the State can be set off with unquestionable debts owed and due to the State or its entities. This is a salutary provision for the debtors of the State.

Under international law foreign governments and their sovereigns, diplomatic bodies and international institutions and their staff benefit from the same immunity. This is either by virtue of international comity or the provisions of some international instruments such as the Vienna Convention on diplomatic relations 1961 and Vienna Convention on consular relations 1963 and some Head Quarter Agreements. the underlying principle is that states are independent and equal and no state may exercise jurisdiction over another state without its consent and the courts of a state may not assume jurisdiction over another state. Creditors of such entities or persons can only rely on their good faith and the intervention of the receiving state.

Article 32: With the exception of the auction sale of immovable property, execution of a writ may be pursued to term by virtue of a writ of provisional execution.

Execution shall then be carried out at the creditor's risk, in that where the writ is subsequently modified, he shall fully make good any damage caused by the execution, with no room for fault on his part.

Comment:

By virtue of this article a creditor in possession of a writ of provisional writ of execution may carry out forceful execution at his risk and peril. However attachment and sale of landed property may not be carried out in the absence of a final writ of execution as defined in Article 33 below. This is an exception to the principle enunciated in section 31 above.

The question has arisen as to the role of the trial court in staying such execution undertaken pursuant to a provisional writ. The position of the common Court of Justice and Arbitration is that the national courts cannot stay such execution once engaged. In the case of Epoux Karnib v Societe Generale de Banque [de la C]ote d'Ivoire (SGBCI) Arret No 002 du 11 October 2001 the CCJA stated clearly that where the issue before the national court of appeal was one of stay of provisional execution ordered by a lower court, the CCJA was incompetent to entertain an appeal against the decision of the national court of appeal as this was not in relation to a matter dealt with by any of the Uniform Acts.

Although this ratio[nale] was followed by the Court in the subsequent cases of Arrets Nos 12, 13 and 14 of 19 June 2003, i.e., SEHIC Hollywood S.A. v SGBC, SOCOM SARL v SGBC, SOCOM SARL v SGBC & BEAC, the Court however emphasized that where execution has been commenced by virtue of a provisional writ of execution in accordance with Article 32 of the Uniform Act National Courts cannot stop the execution which shall pursue to the end. However national courts remain competent to stay the execution of an order of provisional execution ordered by virtue of Law No 92/008 of 14 August 19992 as amended.

This section has also been misconstrued by certain judges as conferring on them the power to order provisional execution notwithstanding appeal.

Article 49: The competent authority to rule on all disputes or petitions relating to a forced act of performance or seizure for security shall be the president of the court ruling in urgent proceedings, or the judge delegated by him.

His decision may be appealed against within a period of fifteen days from its pronouncement.

The time limit for appeal and the exercise of the right to appeal shall not bar enforcement except in the presence of a contrary well-reasoned decision of the president of the competent court.

Comment:

This provision far from instituting a judge in charge of disputes relating to any means of execution confers new attributions to the President of [the] Court ruling in urgent proceedings or the judge delegated by him. Principally, it provides that the competent authority [shall] rule on all disputes or petition[s] relating to a forced act of performance or sequestration shall be the President of the court ruling in urgent proceedings or the judge delegated by him. The French translation of "the president of the court ruling in urgent proceedings or the judge delegated by him" is "le president de la juridiction statuant en matière d'urgence ou le magistrat délégué par lui". While it is obvious under the Civil law that "le [p]résident de la juridiction statuant en matière d'urgence" is the "Juge [des référés]" in order to render applicable the section 13 of Ordinance 72/4, this [is] not the case with the common law where urgent matters are entertained at all levels by the President of the Court of First Instance, High Court and the Court of Appeal or any Magistrate or Judge delegated by them to that effect.

Despite this confusion, it must be noted here that the President of the Court of First Instance remains solely competent in these[] matters to the exclusion of all other jurisdictions.

Cameroon law No 2003/009 of 10 July 2003 which particularly designates the [C]ourt of First Instance as the competent court in matters of exequatur is a step in the right direction and this precision should be extended to other Uniform Acts.

Another question is how this jurisdiction shall be seized? Should it be motion ex parte or by motion on notice? In every situation the guiding principle is that whenever the interest of a third party will be affected by the measure solicited, such party must be put on notice.

Article 130: Any creditor who fulfils the conditions provided for under Article 91 of this Uniform Act may join a seizure in progress on the properties of the debtor by means of an opposition and carry out, where need be a supplementary seizure.

No opposition may be received after the property has been verified.

Comment:

After the seizure any other creditor in possession of a writ of execution showing a debt due for immediate payment may join the proceedings by way of opposition or extend the first seizure to other goods belonging to the debtor.

The first debtor may also oppose where he possesses a new writ of execution against the debtor or where he intends to attach other goods belonging to the debtor. In both cases the debtor must be served with the opposition[.]

The opposition must be done before the inventory of the goods under Article 124 under pain of foreclosure.

CCJA - Rules of Procedure

Article 19: The seat of the Court shall be in Abidjan. However, the Court may, if it deems necessary, meet in other places on the territory of any member State with the prior consent of such State which shall under no circumstances be involved financially.

Index

Printed in the United Kingdom by
Lightning Source UK Ltd., Milton Keynes
141674UK00001B/2/P

9 781846 731501